Previous page: Larry Phillips accepts his award at the NASCAR Winston Racing Series banquet in 1991 in Nashville, Tennessee. Photo used courtesy of the Judy Phillips collection.

LARRY PHILLIPS
NASCAR'S ONLY FIVE-TIME
WINSTON RACING SERIES CHAMPION
MASTER OF THE SHORT TRACK

KENDALL BELL
DAVID ZESZUTEK

LARRY PHILLIPS: NASCAR's ONLY FIVE-TIME WINSTON RACING SERIES CHAMPION; MASTER OF THE SHORT TRACK
ISBN 978-1-933523-95-8

For more information contact Bella Rosa Books, P.O. Box 4251 CRS, Rock Hill, SC 29732. Or online at www.bellarosebooks.com

First printing: January 2011

Library of Congress Control Number: 2010935827

Printed in the United States of America on acid-free paper.

Cover design by First Impressions Printing and Design, Springfield, Missouri www.fiprint.net

Front cover photos courtesy of Dan Mahoney.

Back cover photo by Kevin Vandivier.

This book is dedicated to Judy Phillips, wife of Larry Phillips, NASCAR's only Five-Time Winston Racing Series Champion. Judy has been wonderful in helping us put this book together. Without her assistance, it would not have been possible. Her unconditional love and support was one of the keys to Larry's continued success. She inspired us to never give up on pursuing our dreams. For this, we will always be grateful.

TABLE OF CONTENTS

Larry Phillips gives his trademark smile from inside his No. 75 race car.

FOREWORD

Larry Phillips was authentic.

The word "authentic" and the name "Larry Phillips" complement one another.

He was passionate about his racing. Never mind that he operated his race shop and motorsports equipment shop for a living. The part of his work he loved most was getting behind the wheel of a stock car with the number 75 on the side.

He introduced applications of his knowledge at the track. He'd look at the starting line-ups on the pit board and formulate his race plan, plotting every other driver's likely race style right down to their lines on the track. He envisioned the whole race and generally knew exactly how the race would unfold.

All that computer-based technology that has come into the sport since Larry stopped racing—Larry had it all in his head—he knew a car's balance by its feel.

I've written that Larry was an "acquired taste." The more time spent with him led to increasing appreciation of him. In that regard, his wife Judy is one of the luckiest people in the world, as is his racing son, Terry.

The first time I walked into Larry's old shop on Commercial Street in Springfield, he was sweeping the floor and wasn't much impressed by a kid from NASCAR and a photographer from the series sponsor. He kept sweeping.

Over the years of covering his five NASCAR national championships and a couple that got away, Larry thought me to be credible, a little protective of him, and we were friends. He knew I wouldn't waste his time, and I'd try to help him through his most uncomfortable experiences ... accepting his honors and all the fanfare with which NASCAR surrounds its weekly series national champion.

And over that decade, as I've written, (his wife) Judy just got more beautiful with every championship.

I'm glad Terry is still going strong racing. Not a week goes by that I don't scan the trade papers for his name to keep track of his career. And to this day, not a week goes by that I don't think of something Larry said or did, or his sometimes self-depreciating sense of humor—his "sparkling personality" he'd refer to—for which he thought he was known.

L.P. was multi-dimensional, though. He'd loan parts or give advice to anyone in need at the track. He mentored more drivers and crewmen than a lot of us can remember … at least a couple of generations of them. And he'd spend time after the races signing autographs for sincerely adoring fans. That's when you could see him lose his "race face" and actually smile on a winning night.

I love this book because, like Larry, it's authentic. It will draw you into the life and times of a special person. Enjoy.

Paul Schaefer
NASCAR media coordinator
Daytona Beach, Florida
June 25, 2009

NASCAR collection

Larry Phillips, right, and his pit crew in the Winner's Circle at Lebanon I-44 Speedway in Lebanon, Missouri.

LARRY PHILLIPS

NASCAR'S ONLY FIVE-TIME
WINSTON RACING SERIES CHAMPION

MASTER OF THE SHORT TRACK

SPRINGFIELD, MISSOURI FAIRGROUNDS

CONOCO 100

100 LAP FEATURE
½ mile SPEEDWAY

LIMITED CUBIC INCH ENGINE

STOCK CAR

National Championship

Gen. Adm. – $3.00   4,000 SEATS HELD FOR SALE AT TRACK
FOR $3.50 RESERVED OR BOX SEATS CALL 417 833–2660

$1,500 TO WIN

COURTESY OF

Love OIL CO.

ONLY THE FASTEST 22 CARS MAKE THE 100 LAP RACE.

QUALIFYING: SAT. NITE, SEPT. 5

CHAMPIONSHIP: 8 PM, SUN., SEPT. 6

RAIN DATE: 8 P.M., MON,
SEPT. 7, (LABOR DAY)

Fairgrounds Speedway's promotional poster for the Conoco 100, featuring Larry Phillips' No. 75 car on the cover.

CHAPTER ONE
A Star Is Born

Larry Phillips was born July 3, 1942, in Springfield, Missouri, a son of Jim and Margie Phillips, who were farmers. He attended Bois D'Arc grade school and Parkview High School in Springfield. If his classmates and teachers gave his future any thought at all, they might have assumed he would spend his life on a tractor. But Larry was anything but the typical young man. He had a passion for speed.

About 1960, he began racing regularly at the Fairgrounds Speedway in Springfield, and everything he learned was by trial and error. He wasn't one to seek advice. He taught himself how to race—and how to win.

The NASCAR Winston Racing Series national champion is the only driver to win the title five times.

Larry was known for being a tough competitor and intimidator on the track. But his willingness to help younger drivers made him a favorite of those eager to learn. He was a mentor to many drivers who went on to make a name for themselves including Rusty Wallace, Mark Martin, and Kenny Wallace as well as noted crew chief James Ince. Among his friends were established NASCAR drivers Dick Trickle and Russ Wallace.

Larry Phillips at the age of three in 1945.

But Judy Phillips says there was another side of her husband the general public never saw. He was soft-hearted and caring.

His family taught him good manners and took him to the Clear Creek Baptist Church every Sunday, Wednesday, or anytime there was a service, she said.

Judy said Larry learned his work ethic from his dad working on the family farm. And that ethic was to always work hard despite the circumstances.

"He was playing, fell out of a tree and broke his arm and his dad made him drive the tractor the next day anyway," she said.

His dad also made Larry drive the truck to the feed store when he was about seven years old, but there was a big problem: He couldn't see over the steering wheel, and the store was on the other side of a busy highway, the now famous Route 66.

"He would steer and then climb down and change gears," Judy said. "Then he'd quickly jump back up to where he could see to steer."

The family lived in Casper, Wyoming, for a short time. Larry's mother wanted him to take violin lessons. But Larry never got past, "Mary Had a Little Lamb" on the violin. He also had a paper route.

"Jim (Larry's dad) went to church, too, as long as Margie (Jim's wife) was alive. As long as she was alive everybody went to church. Unfortunately, she later committed suicide. Larry was only twelve at the time."

Judy said Larry's mother Margie's death had a profound effect on the entire family.

"Everything stopped," Judy said. "They stopped celebrating Christmas and Larry's family stopped going to church. It just wasn't the same."

Even though Larry's father raised him after his mother's death, Joe Naegler, a longtime friend and fellow racer, said Larry's mother Margie also left her mark on the young man.

"I would say that his mother

Larry Phillips playing his violin in his Casper, Wyoming, home. Larry's mother wanted him to be a violinist, but he had other ideas.

had a lot of influence on him. Joe said he didn't think Larry's mother would have allowed him to quit school, but her death had a dramatic affect on him.

"I think his dad recognized his passion for racing; it got him calmed down and gave him direction in his life. So his dad was very supportive of that and it worked out pretty well as time went on."

Judy said she met Larry in 1970, although she had watched him race for several years before that.

She said she finally met Larry one night at a restaurant but neither one made a very good first impression.

Jim Phillips, left, with his son, Larry Phillips.

"I really don't remember his first words but I thought he was … just a smart aleck," she said. "We sat there for a while and talked and I think I might have been bad mouthing him maybe just a little because I really wasn't a Larry Phillips fan."

After that, Judy began noticing Larry more often.

"We ran into each other, just every now and then," she said.

Larry finally asked Judy out on a date.

And that was the beginning of a long relationship.

"We dated and lived together off and on for eleven years then finally thought we knew each other well enough to get married," Judy Phillips said.

The couple married on November 20, 1981, and began building a lifetime of memories together.

Even at the tender age of seven in 1949, Larry Phillips had already started working on his charismatic smile.

CHAPTER TWO
Remembering a Friend

"Larry was friends with (famed NASCAR driver) Ken Schrader's dad," Judy Phillips said. "They met at the race track in Fenton, Missouri, just outside of St. Louis.

"I don't think Larry really taught Kenny how to race," she said, "but they were buddies and rode dirt bikes and motorcycles, and talked about stock car racing, among other things and Larry would tell him what he thought he should do. But I really don't remember Schrader whenever he was younger. It was mostly Mark Martin and Rusty Wallace."

Larry Phillips, left, and NASCAR great Ken Schrader just before a race at I-70 Speedway in Odessa, Missouri.

Judy said Rusty never worked for Larry but raced with him.

"Yeah, he would come down from St. Louis," she said. "Larry was friends with Rusty's dad."

"[Future NASCAR star] Mark [Martin] came up and worked with Larry," she said.

"That was Mark's father's doing," she said. "He wanted Mark to see what racing was all about from the ground up. So he sent him up here for I think it was two summers in a row."

"I remember when he graduated high school, he came up here and worked for a couple of winters, just to learn stuff," said Larry's son, Terry Phillips. "He was just like the rest of us, and not necessarily just sweeping floors—everybody did that. There was one boss, and that was LP (Larry Phillips). He always said, 'There ain't no crew chiefs, I'm the crew chief.'"

Mark Martin said he remembers those times well.

Mark and his dad, Julian, started preparing for the 1975 season on Thanksgiving Day 1974 with the bare chassis from a 1955 Chevrolet.

They carried it to Springfield where Larry, already known as one of the top short-track stock car drivers in the Midwest, welded a roll cage onto it. Mark said this was his first visit to a professional race shop. It was also the first meeting between Mark and Larry—but it wouldn't be the last.

The first time the drivers met on the track was in late 1976, when Mark brought his late model car—a Camaro—to the Fairgrounds Speedway in Springfield, Larry Phillips' home track. And this car had a 496 cubic-inch Chevrolet V-8 engine. Even though the car was built for racing on dirt and the track was asphalt, Mark said he didn't have a choice; this was the only car he had.

Larry had been so dominant at the track that track promoters often hired top regional and national drivers to try to beat him. On this particular night, NASCAR Winston Cup star Donnie Allison was that driver.

Although the three drivers—Larry, Mark and Donnie—all started at the back, it took only three laps for each one to come through the pack. Larry led the next twenty-seven laps, with Mark pushing his car to its limit trying to keep up. But on lap thirty-one, Mark's engine blew and Larry went on to win.

On April 10, 1977, the second race of the 1977 season at Fairgrounds Speedway, Mark was back.

This poster is popular around the Ozarks. The caption reads "Hey Larry, Do you think I'll ever be as good as you?" It shows Larry Phillips (seated) talking with a teenage Mark Martin.

Wisconsin driver Tom Reffner, the winningest short-track driver in 1975, was in town to

Dennis Slane collection

Mark Martin, before he became a household name among NASCAR race fans, with his ASA Camaro at the Fairgrounds Speedway in Springfield, Missouri.

battle with Larry.

Tom might as well have stayed home as the highly touted duel turned out to be between Mark and Larry. The drivers stayed door to door during the heat races with Larry edging Mark at the line to take the pole in the main feature.

In the feature, Mark took the lead on the fifth lap and stayed there, with Larry right behind him all the way to the checkered flag.

Even though he lost the race, Larry knew it wasn't a fluke.

"We had no problem," he was quoted as saying after the race. "We just got outrun."

A few years later Larry reflected on that night.

"[Mark's] fan following was enormous because they already have a guy—me—who everybody hates. Or at least half the people hate. Mark was everybody's idol, especially with him being a youngster and his mild manner. Mark had a little different style that he'd run on the track. It was a little wider line. Coming off the corners, he was just right there against the fence. He just used every bit of the race track. A couple of times he outran me like this. And I thought I'd better follow him. I never did feel comfortable with it but it was fast."

And even though they were fierce competitors on the track, the friendship grew.

One night, Mark had caused Larry to crash. And after the race, Mark and his crew went to Larry's shop. At first there were cold stares. Larry's crew didn't want to see the driver who had just cost them a chance at another win. Mark's crew stood around the wall and started handing tools and other parts to Larry's crew. Eventually, the teams worked all night to rebuild Larry's car.

Mark knew he was learning from the best. But learning about racing piecemeal wasn't enough. The youngster wanted more.

It was after Mark graduated from high school that he took a job working at Larry's shop. He had an apartment and worked all week and then met his own team at the track on Friday nights.

Mark said the experience was more valuable than he could have imagined. He eventually learned to build different parts for the cars and became a better welder and fabricator.

> *"The first job I gave him was gutting out an old Camaro body, scraping the tar out and cutting it up."*
> —**Larry Phillips talking about hiring Mark Martin, who later became a popular NASCAR driver, when Martin was only a teenager.**

Larry later remembered Mark as quite a worker:

"The first job I gave him was gutting out an old Camaro body, scraping the tar out and cutting it up," he said in an interview a few years later. "It was hot work. But he just stayed right there with her. We were kind of testing him. And if I'd been him, I would have gone home."

And Mark Martin wasn't the only future NASCAR star to visit Larry's shop.

Russ Wallace brought his sons, Rusty and Kenny, to visit Larry, but his middle son, Michael, rarely went along.

"Mike really didn't hang around Rusty and little Kenny," Judy said. "He didn't go racing with them that I can remember. It was mainly Mark and Rusty that Larry helped."

Helping his friends became a way Larry dealt with the tremendous stress of trying to win. Judy said it actually helped make things easier.

"[Rusty] Wallace was so funny," she said. "But when it came to racing, all the funny business stopped. You know they could clown around and stuff at the shop, as long as the work got done. But when it was time to race, you better get to racing."

Dennis Slane collection

Larry Phillips, No. 75, and Mark Martin, No. 2, battle it out at the Fairgrounds Speedway in Springfield, Missouri.

Larry Phillips, who was always hands-on with his car, adjusts the setup for a race in California during the 1970s.

CHAPTER THREE
NASCAR Stars Reflect

Rusty Wallace said it was actually his father, Russ, who introduced him to Larry.

"My father was a short-track dirt race-car driver," he said. "We bought a car from Larry, and Dad won a lot of races with it."

Wallace said when he was about twenty-one years old, Larry began teaching him about race cars.

Dennis Slane collection

RUSTY WALLACE

"I started hanging out at his shop," he said. "He taught me how important it was to know your race car. He taught me a lot about racing."

Wallace said he loved watching Larry race.

"Larry was amazing," he said. "We used to race at the Springfield Fairgrounds—Larry, Mark Martin and me always seemed to race one-two-three.

"I'd look out my left-hand window and Larry would be passing on the left. I'd be passing on the right. Either he'd be leading or I'd be leading."

But it was restarts Wallace said he recalls most fondly.

"He'd do these restarts that would make you gasp," Wallace said.

He said Larry would go full throttle to get a jump on the restarts and if anyone—or anything—was in his way, it better move.

"Mark Martin would say, 'You guys are crazy to do that,'" Wallace said.

Wallace said Larry focused on racing.

"He'll always be known as a guy who didn't have a lot of patience," Rusty said. "He was so focused on cars you knew not to bother him."

But that didn't stop some people from trying.

"A guy came up to him and bothered him while Larry was working," Rusty said. Larry listened until he couldn't take it any more. "Finally, Larry flipped him a quarter and said, 'Call

Dennis Slane collection

Larry Phillips, left, accepts the Legends Award from NASCAR racing great Rusty Wallace at Ozarks Area Racers' Association banquet in 2001 in Springfield, Missouri.

someone who cares.'"

Rusty said Larry was a versatile driver.

"He could win on big oval tracks or little tracks," he said. "He was just one helluva guy. I said probably only him and A.J. Foyt could adapt to so many cars and be successful."

Rusty said he was finally able to let Larry know how much he appreciated all of his help.

"It was at one of the NASCAR functions," he said. "Larry came up; my NASCAR career was skyrocketing. Larry congratulated me. I said, 'I couldn't have done it without you.'"

KEN SCHRADER

"The first time I saw Larry I was just a pup. It would have been like '67. I was twelve. He came down to St. Louis and kicked everybody's butts at the races. That's how I got to know him."

"I didn't 'know' him; I just knew who he was," Ken said. "I started racing in '71 and the car

I started in, a 1964 Impala, we had gotten from Jerry Sifford, who had become good friends with Larry. Over the years, they had become real good friends, and Larry had helped him a lot."

Ken said it was through Jerry that he actually became friends with Larry.

"Jerry and I went down to Springfield and went motorcycle riding with him, maybe about 1969 or so," he said. "I never really knew Larry that close or had any kind of real relationship with him until later."

Ken said Larry drove for him once and the two instantly became great friends.

"About '91 we had an ASA (American Speed Association) race at I-70 (Speedway) and I had to get my neck operated on and couldn't race," he said. "I called Larry and asked if he'd drive the car for me. He went over there and ran the car. That was probably the first time I had spent much time around him.

"When I was sixteen, Jerry and I went out to California and [Larry] was racing out there and I spent about a week around him. But I just sat around on the sideline and kept my mouth shut.

"Larry could be very intense," Ken said. "Larry wasn't racing for love. This was so different from everybody we knew because this wasn't his 'play' on the weekends. It was how he made his living. And that put him in an altogether different position than everybody else."

Ken said Larry made him realize that someone could make a career of racing.

"It was at least a possibility," he said. "Heck, we didn't have anybody out there racing for a living. You didn't even dream about that because that didn't even make sense. But Larry was racing for a living when almost nobody else was doing that on the short tracks."

Ken said Larry later sought him out when Larry couldn't drive one weekend.

"He called me up one time and asked me to run his car," Ken said. "We started knowing each other a little better."

"I didn't spend time around him growing up like Rusty (Wallace) and Mark (Martin) and those guys because I went off open-wheel pavement racing and those guys stayed stock car racing. So I just wasn't really around him."

Ken said he spent more time with Larry after Larry became ill.

"After he was stricken (with cancer) we spent a couple of winters out in Phoenix riding motorcycles and stuff," he said. "I really enjoyed that."

Ken said his experiences with Larry were different each time because the situations were so different.

"I enjoyed the heck out of hanging around him in California. But it wasn't until years later when we were riding motorcycles together and you knew him and could actually talk with him."

Judy Phillips collection

Larry Phillips, left, and NASCAR great Ken Schrader just before a race at I-70 Speedway in Odessa, Missouri.

Larry first came over from Springfield, Missouri, to Lake Hill in the early seventies. He came in and set a track record, started last in the feature and was in the lead on the first lap, but then dropped a drive shaft.

"He had our attention," Ken said. "When he came back the next week, he was told that his car's body was too rough-looking for our nice track, so he returned the following week with a new body and set another track record before he won the feature.

"When he came back again, they told him the car was too light. Never mind that we didn't have any scales. So, they made him bolt on some old cylinder heads as ballast—sort of like adding an anchor—but it didn't matter. He was the best. "Everybody started buying stuff from him because they couldn't beat him."

Ken recalls with a smile one of his earliest and fondest memories of Larry.

"I was only thirteen when Jerry Sifford (one of the earliest influences on Ken's racing career) took me to Springfield to run a four-hour motorcycle race. I ran the mandatory, non-stop hour with a hole in my knee after I fell. I ended up needing six stitches later.

"After the race, Larry gave me a screwdriver—the drink, not the tool—and suddenly I didn't feel so bad. But even though it didn't hurt anymore, the knee got really stiff and swollen on me, so I had to go to the emergency room. [It was a] pretty big deal to have Larry Phillips carry you into the hospital.

"He wasn't a warm, fuzzy kind of guy," Ken said. "He went to the race track to win, not to get fans and friends, but he did okay on that, too. He'd build you a new car and then he would beat you. If you didn't like that, hell, he would beat you again. I mean, you were gonna' get beat.

"There was a group mainly composed of senior citizens that would follow him to tracks and they were called the "Cowbell Brigade," Ken said.

These were not only his biggest fans but they kept a record of everything he did on the track in writing along with other drivers—notebooks full of statistics, pictures and mementos. Larry was glad to hear the cowbell when he went out onto the track. They rang it when he was on the track and all the fans knew why they were there: to see Larry win.

"I wish he was still here," Ken said. "Larry got his career taken away by off-track illness. When Larry passed away, it created another big hole in racing that will never be filled. He wasn't an easy guy to get to know or like, but he was a big influence because his career proved that you could go racing full time. Larry taught me that you could leave the track with money.

> *"He wasn't a warm, fuzzy kind of guy. He went to the race track to win, not to get fans and friends, but he did okay on that, too. He'd build you a new car and then he would beat you. If you didn't like that, hell, he would beat you again. I mean, you were gonna' get beat."*
>
> **—Ken Schrader, NASCAR driver**

"Larry was never anything but helpful when I went to him with questions," Ken said. "But you knew if you asked him a dumb question, you knew what kind of answer you were going to get.

"We spent those last couple of winters out in Arizona riding motorcycles a bunch," he said. "And we weren't there just to ride motorcycles. They'd have some dirt races at Casa Grande. I was running a car. And he was out there with some of his buddies because (Larry's son) Terry Gene was running. I really didn't have to work on my car in the daytime. I had guys to do it. So Larry and I, as buddies, would go up and ride our bikes.

"He was like one of those guys that have Nextel Championships behind their name and come across as being the total hard-ass guy—which they are on the racetrack. They've got big hearts to help out. They just don't want anyone to know it."

MARK MARTIN

"Always good times with Larry and always exciting," Mark said. "He gave me my first job after high school. Larry was a piece of work. He had no other employees at the time. The first assignment that he gave me was to build upper A-frames. Larry left me alone and stayed in his office."

Mark said the work was difficult, but he got better and more acquainted with building the race cars during each week.

"The first year I raced with Larry, he was a tough competitor and a bit slippery. I can recall racing with him at the Fairgrounds Speedway. Larry was running second and can remember Larry had a cigarette hanging out of the side of his mouth. He threw the cigarette down and beat me. Larry influenced me as a driver because he was very intense when he was competing."

Mark said the best way to describe Larry is that he was comical.

MARK MARTIN

"When you weren't expecting it, he'd do or say something that would crack everyone up," he said.

How good was Larry?

"He was the only driver I'd pay to watch race," Mark said.

KENNY WALLACE

NASCAR Nextel Cup Driver Kenny Wallace, brother of Rusty Wallace and syndicated national television's "Speed" commentator, also has fond memories of Larry Phillips.

"I met him through my dad, Russ," Kenny said. "We're from St. Louis, and Dad raced against Larry. They were good friends."

Kenny said the relationship soon spilled over into business.

"Larry started building our race cars in his shop in Springfield," he said.

He said this was well before he was old enough to drive.

"I was only six or seven years old," he said. "I was the youngest one and I thought Larry was a god."

Going to the track to watch Larry race was one of the things Kenny loved to do.

"He was so good they'd put a bounty on him," Kenny said. "They'd offer like five-hundred dollars to anyone who could beat him. I don't think I ever saw him lose."

He said the Phillips family became lifelong friends with the Wallaces. He also said he admires what Larry was able to do.

"The older I got, the more I looked up to him," he said. "He took it seriously. It's how he made a living. There's a handful of drivers: Dick Trickle, Richie Evans (a three-time Modified Race of Champions winner) and Larry Phillips; they raced for a living when other people said there was no way you could do that."

Kenny said Larry did more with less than anyone he had ever known.

He learned early on how serious Larry could be a about racing.

"If he was talking to you and someone interrupted him, Larry would look at them and say, 'Here's a quarter. Go call someone who cares. I don't have time to talk to you now.'

"There's a saying, 'I have so many wonderful qualities it's easy to overlook my few disturbing habits.' My mom bought me that T-shirt.

"That's how Larry was. The good outweighed the bad," he said.

KENNY WALLACE

Even though he was from St. Louis, Kenny feels a kindred spirit with Larry who lived at the opposite end of the state in Springfield.

"We actually lived in Rolla for a time," Kenny said. "But we're all Ozark people. We all want to beat each other. You don't like it when they beat your ass but you respect them."

The last time Kenny saw Larry was in 2004 at the I-55 Speedway.

"He was sick but he was still Larry," Kenny said. "Of course, you couldn't expect anything less than that. He always wanted to be a winner no matter what the battle—and he was."

The Fox Network had approached Kenny about being a television color commentator. He was undecided but knew who to go to for advice.

"They offered me a lot of money," Kenny said. "I went to Larry for advice. I asked him, 'Should I do TV or keep pursuing my (Winston) Cup dream?'"

Larry told him what he already knew.

"He said, 'You can't do TV; you're a race car driver,'" Kenny said. "He put me at peace about it. They ended up hiring Darrell Waltrip."

RODNEY COMBS

Former NASCAR driver Rodney Combs, who was inducted into the National Dirt Late Model Hall of Fame in 2001, said he met Larry around 1974 or '75.

Rodney said the racers were fierce competitors on the track, but off the track they were friends.

"Both of us ran dirt in the '80s because that was big money, and we ran off and on in Missouri. Our sons were friends with each other and would slot race."

The drivers often discussed racing strategy.

"Larry was very creative and taking the car and doing his own magic to it and coming up with traction," Rodney said. "We bounced ideas off of each other. We figured it was a better way to go fast.

"Larry was serious about racing," Rodney said. "He was a one-man band at the time. Whether it was pavement or dirt, he figured out ways to go faster and was very good driver. He was always on top of his game. We were able to win our share wherever we raced and hit it off."

NDRA was paying huge payouts at the time and both Rodney and Larry made the best of it.

"(In 1979 or '80) NDRA was paying ten-thousand dollars to win," he said. "We jumped into it because it was big money and a big circuit. Larry also raced in the NCRA Circuit from Missouri."

Rodney was always impressed with Larry's versatility.

"Racing was his living," Rodney said. "Larry was very creative. He was a pure racer. He could build them and he could drive them. He was a great racer, a great individual. He was one of the top racers in the country. He could do it all."

NAME-BRAND EQUIPMENT

Both Rodney and Larry tried to run only the best parts in their cars. One of the drivers' favorites was equipment made by Howe Racing.

"We ran Howe (racing equipment) in our pavement car," he said. "Howe Racing was one of the most respected drivers and chassis builders. A lot of people had that design."

> "Larry was serious about racing. He was a one-man band at the time. Whether it was pavement or dirt, he figured out ways to go faster and was very good driver. He was always on top of his game."
>
> **—Rodney Combs, NASCAR driver**

Rodney drove for Howe Racing for three or four years then he started making his own chassis, and became quite successful with the endeavor.

"We built them out of Springfield. We sold a lot of cars, even in Australia, he said. But Larry liked a chassis made by a different company better.

"Larry raced all kinds of difference chassis. Late eighties and early nineties Larry raced Mastersbilt (chassis)."

But he said Larry could modify the chassis to his own specifications.

Some of Larry's changes included mono leaf springs, fiberglass arms, toll bars and a lot of different setup combinations.

"He also raced a car with a fifth coil spring in it," Rodney said. "He used a spring or shock or rubber type of cushion. We used a Reese bar or fifth coil without a spring and put a mount in rubber and had a deal on top of the rear end like a slider that we had foam rubber around. That's what accounted for all the innovative devices to try to make the car grip in slicker conditions. We didn't run week-to-week; we just ran the big shows. He did his thing and I did mine, so we were able to use each other's ideas to make the cars better."

As the friendship grew, so did the trust that came with sharing information.

"We exchanged a lot of ideas," he said. "We didn't share everything, but we shared a lot. We would talk about different ideas. The neatest thing he ever told me was about that fifth coil under the frame."

Rodney said Larry sometimes used unorthodox methods to experiment with different setups and equipment. He said one of those times involved Larry's then-young son Terry.

"He asked Terry to get under the car and take the sheet metal off the side of the car. Terry hung over the car to watch the fifth coil spring action as he went around the track. Larry wanted to know exactly what the spring was doing no matter what speed he was going."

DICK TRICKLE VERSUS LARRY PHILLIPS

Nationally, probably only a few fans cared, but around the Ozarks, one of the big debates was whether Larry or Dick Trickle—Larry's longtime rival from Wisconsin—was the better driver. Dick was known as being someone hard to beat—just like Larry. The question became fodder for many arguments around many tracks through the years.

James Ince, Larry's longtime crew chief, said common feeling among other short-track drivers was that Dick had the record for the most victories. Larry respected Dick and wouldn't disparage a driver he held in such high esteem. Larry called him Superman. When anyone asked Larry how many races he won, he'd always answer, "Just a few less than Dick Trickle."

Rodney said comparing the records of Dick Trickle and Larry Phillips is like comparing apples to oranges.

"Dick Trickle did all his winning on the pavement whereas Larry did as much winning on the pavement as on dirt," he said.

Rodney said that, in his opinion, Larry won as many or more races than Dick.

"It takes a great racer to win both on dirt and pavement as he did," Rodney said. "[Larry] is one great race car driver. He was a proven racer and could drive fast no matter what condition, pavement or dirt. He was all about winning and being creative. He could make any changes or build his own."

"You could race him side by side and you did not know where he was going to be. He was very precise whether he was building the car or driving the race car. It was all about winning."

Joe Naegler agreed.

Joe said Dick was the only driver at the time he would compare to being equal to Larry.

"Trickle was probably as good as Larry every time we saw him," Joe said. "And he probably beat us more than we beat him, but he was a hell of a racer and he was in the same caliber as Larry—and in his part of the world, he was well known. I don't think Trickle loaded up and went to Florida and he didn't go to Colorado or to the West Coast. That's the different things that Larry did. Larry went into other areas of the country and competed in events with the local guys that were real good. Trickle stayed basically in Wisconsin, Minnesota, and then he got over into Illinois some. But more of his racing, until he got in Missouri, was in Minnesota and Wisconsin and Michigan. But [Dick Trickle] was one hell of a good racer."

And fans got an opportunity to see for themselves which driver was better. Former driver Rick Sharp said one night a group of people got together and put money up to try to find a driver to beat Larry. "Ten people each put in one-hundred dollars and paid Dick Trickle a thousand dollars to race," Rick said. "Dick beat him. Larry went up to the press box and announced over the loudspeaker, 'If you had asked, I could have told you I can't beat Trickle. I'd have saved you a whole lot of money.'"

CHAPTER FOUR
A Driver's Son Remembers

Terry Phillips, Larry's only son, said he wanted to be a driver like his dad and started working toward that at a young age.

"Pretty much, I just always wanted to be (a driver). But working on his stuff and starting too young, sometimes you get in bad habits, so I think I started when I was nineteen or twenty."

Although Larry never encouraged him to drive, Terry knew it was something he wanted to do.

Terry's first race was at the former Airport Speedway (now Springfield Raceway) in Springfield, Missouri, in 1986.

Terry said his dad helped him prepare the car and was there for his first race.

"I set the car up pretty much myself, but he kind of oversaw it," Terry said. "But the first night I got in the thing, I had to start in the back and wallow around the speedway fairly slow. I remember I blew a radiator hose out and spun out, and the field was about to lap me, and I think I spun out on the backstretch. The water hose blew off and I thought I was dying. I thought everybody was going to run over me.

Dan Mahoney collection

Terry Phillips, son of Larry Phillips, poses beside his Late Model dirt car.

"Then in the next race I told him what I thought was wrong and made some changes," Terry said. "I'd been racing go-carts, and the thing just steered so slow for me, so I did some chassis changes, and started on the pole the next week at the Monett Speedway, in Monett, Missouri."

Larry wanted to make sure Terry didn't finish last.

"He'd run out there on the back straightaway and tell me when to start, when to go, and made things a little embarrassing for me. I kind of thought I knew what I was doing; evidently I didn't," Terry said with a laugh.

Larry was somewhat of a perfectionist. Although Terry didn't like it at the time, he later came to realize his dad was right.

"Well, it certainly was his way … and it was probably right, but he had a certain way of wanting things done and expected them done that way. As I have gotten older, I'm glad he was that way. I mean, now we work pretty hard around here. It isn't near as stressful now as it was back then. We still have good work ethics and the cars are done before we get to the race track, so it taught me a lot as far as work ethic goes."

Some people have asked Terry if the competition was fierce to beat his dad on the track.

"Oh, no," he said. "I mean, like him, I want to beat everybody out there. I didn't race with him that much. We didn't race against each other a whole lot. He went and ran asphalt and I stayed with dirt.

"He won everything, I guess you'd say. He worked hard. It wasn't given to him," Terry said. "He started on his own, you know, back in the day they built everything; built and sold cars and parts. He was way ahead of his time and had a unique will to win, no matter what it took. As far as his personal life to anything … he sacrificed everything for his cars and those races every night."

Terry said he and his dad had a good relationship.

"Yeah, we were real close, actually," Terry said. "You know a lot of people didn't see that because, at the track, he was in the zone and focused. We probably didn't have what you'd call a 'father-son relationship' like a lot of people. He was kind of the boss, but we'd still talk about cars or whatever, and like I said, now that I'm older looking back, he tried to talk to me. Especially there at the end, we talked a whole lot then about more personal stuff like religion and things like that, and we got really close."

THE LATER YEARS

Terry said Larry wouldn't open up to many people, but that changed near the end of his life.

"That's probably when he did most of his talking. He was a little confused about things, not that I know everything, but we believed in the same direction. Then he still had questions. I guess when you're dying you have questions and I just gave him my opinion about what I thought was going to happen, or what it was, and I think it helped him quite a bit at the end. He had some things in his life that made him doubt, but I think he really got right (with God) at the end."

Terry said there was a side of his father that few ever saw.

"He was a really emotional person and nobody ever saw that," Terry said. "People saw him mad a lot because that is the only thing he would show. He would get sad easy. He would get upset, but he wouldn't let it show. I think it had something to do with his childhood. Things happened in his life, and he just wasn't going to let anybody see that side of him."

Terry said Larry reached just about every goal he ever set for himself.

"He always knew exactly what he was going to do and the way he was going to do it; whether it was building his shop or building a race car; he could do anything. I always tell people he was

Dan Mahoney collection

Larry Phillips in his asphalt car—a Camaro.

borderline genius. He would build helicopters, airplanes, just anything. He was into it a hundred percent and he got it done right, probably better than what it was supposed to be. He would see things wrong and fix it. I would say that he did everything he ever wanted to do."

Terry said tension was often high at his dad's shop.

"It was intense and he'd get in a bad mood real easy," he said. "He was a really moody person when he was focused on something and didn't want people to bother him. (He was) trying to sell parts and cars and sometimes it didn't work out too well.

"He was pretty hard on me, but like I told someone, 'It's a little easier at the shop now, but I'd love to take a butt-chewin' any time.' It didn't kill me, just made me stronger. I don't regret any of it. He was hard on me, but it's okay."

Terry said his dad usually underestimated himself. And he did a lot for other people.

"Whether he told them something directly or indirectly, he watched you all the time and saw how you did things, and made the sport better, way better. It took a big leap with him. Without him we wouldn't be near as good racers around this area, and I feel that this area has about the best racers in the country, bar none. Other racers saw how he operated, and they got that same attitude and swagger."

Terry said he can see his father's influence on other drivers.

"It's been a long time since I've been around Rusty, but I really recognize that attitude and that drive to win. I can see it in him and Mark (Martin) and a lot of people who have come through here. Anybody who's been around him is more intense. I'm probably the most laid back one of them all. Like I told him before he passed away, I've learned so much from him, not just racing.

"He said, 'You know I wasn't a real good dad.' I told him, 'You were a fine dad.' You look back and see what to do and what not to do and that taught me a lot. I just hope people recognize him for him and what he brought to the sport."

Bob & Loretta Williams collection

Larry Phillips in 1985.

CHAPTER FIVE
The Early Years

When Larry was about fifteen years old, he met Joe Naegler. The Naeglers—brothers Joe, Steven and Richard and their father, Bill—became good friends with Larry.

Joe, a fellow racer, said he remembered that first meeting well.

"I was sixteen. That's when we met each other," Joe said. "I was working for his dad, and we were taking down houses, a board at a time. His dad kept telling me about his boy, 'The Boy' he'd call him.

"One day I was up on a house in Springfield by myself and his dad wasn't there, and a big kid walked up in the yard, and I was up on the roof, and he looked up at me and said, 'Well, you must be Joe.' And I said, 'Yeah. And you're Larry … I've heard of you.' He said, 'Well, I've heard of you, too.' Anyway, we just hit it off, first time I ever saw him, we became instant buddies you might say.

"I believe it was about 1958. We just became fast friends and we were out running around town and we just stayed close."

Joe said Larry's father was a man to admire.

"Larry's dad was really nice fellow," Joe said. "He came from humble beginnings and lived out on a farm that his mother and dad, at some time, had bought out toward Bois D'Arc and he was a country man. At that time, if you had an eighth-grade education, that was pretty good. He was good with math and had a good vocabulary, and he got along with people very well and was a good communicator, and a straight shooter. Whatever he said was his word. He didn't put out any BS. If he told you something, that was the way it was and he never backed down.

"Larry's dad never had much money, per se, but they were always supportive of Larry's racing," Joe said. "His dad bought the cars and paid the bills, and it was the only thing that Larry had that he'd gotten a hold of that kept him motivated and … that was about the only thing he had any interest in."

Joe said the year after he and Larry met, the duo discovered stock cars.

"We went out to the fair grounds for the fair, and we could hear the sprint race cars running over there. I think that same week, toward the end of the week, they had a stock car race, and we went to the races. I can still remember it. Larry said, 'We've got to have one of those.'"

Bob & Loretta Williams collection

Larry Phillips and Loretta Williams, trophy queen at Fairgrounds Speedway beside his car at the Springfield, Missouri, track.

Judy Phillips said Larry "borrowed" his first race car.

"He went to his dad's car lot, which he was not supposed to do, and took one of his dad's cars to the race track," she said. "And the first turn he wrecked the car. He got in big trouble when he brought the car back."

But perhaps for the first time in his life, Larry had discovered something he really wanted to do.

Joe said Larry realized he needed a car of his own if he was to be competitive. So he worked hard, saved his money and bought one.

"The first one that Larry had was from a guy named Kenny Smith," Joe said. "Kenny worked in a service station over on Sunshine Street in Springfield. They weren't real stock cars, but if you put a roll cage in it and take the interior out and change the spring in the right front, that was a stock car."

"Kenny Smith worked at night and had taken a chisel and a hammer and cut all the interior sheet metal out and gutted it. That was the first car Larry drove. It was a Buick, I believe, or an Oldsmobile. I can't remember.

"The biggest thing I remember is that the engine blew in it, and if it was an Oldsmobile, they put a Buick engine in it, and if it was a Buick, they put an Oldsmobile engine in it," Joe said. "For that year, they had so many cars—they had over a hundred cars at the Fairgrounds Speedway in

Bob & Loretta Williams collection

Larry Phillips' 1968 Camaro parked behind his shop on Commercial Street in Springfield, Missouri.

Springfield. And I guess it was probably like a feature, and Larry won it. Somebody protested because he had the wrong engine in the car. You see, at the time there were no (racing) stars. It cost a lot of money to participate and it was mostly old cars."

Joe said the exorbitant salaries paid to today's drivers didn't exist at the time, and no one could have imagined the millions that drivers demand today.

"I think maybe the whole feature paid one-hundred thirty or one-hundred forty dollars or something like that to win," he said.

"I can remember in 1963 or '64, Don Kordallis was the one that won the feature in the heat race and the trophy race, and he won three-hundred ninety-nine dollars and someone gave him a dollar so it would be four-hundred dollars for the winner. That was a lot of money—four-hundred dollars to win on Friday night."

"The place was packed with people, and we were supposed to get forty percent of the take, so I don't think [admission] cost was much more than a dollar twenty-five or a dollar fifty at the most, so that was considered big money at that time."

Joe said even though the money was important, that's not what motivated Larry.

"Early on, we weren't thinking about the money so much. We were thinking about the race," he said. "You know … primarily most people [who] would be good at any kind of sport, would go to win, and then the money came later. If you go for the money, you never win. That was the same on this deal. I mean, we didn't even think about the money; we just had to be at the race. That's the way we saw it anyway."

Judy said Larry had been looking for a used hauler for his race car and finally found one. But it didn't turn out to be quite the deal Larry had first imagined: "Larry had been looking for a hauler in the racing paper," she said. "He went to Webb City [Missouri] to the quarry, because of all of the chat piles that are there, to ride his dirt bike. There were about eight others that went along. About mid-day, Larry came roaring back to the truck and was jumping the hills. He came over a hill, which turned out to be a concrete culvert. He broke a tooth, scraped his chin, and tore a ligament in his arm and collar bone. At first, he tried to laugh it off, but it hurt so bad that he decided to go to the emergency room. The doctor gave him some pills for the pain. Larry could not tolerate pain pills very well. He either got sleepy, hyper or goofy.

"While he was on the pills, he called this guy about a hauler that he wanted to buy. The guy was asking fifty-five hundred dollars for it. Larry talked to him a little bit and then asked the guy what's the least he would take for it. The seller said he would take five thousand dollars and Larry said, 'Hell, the paper said fifty-five hundred' and the seller said, 'Sold!'" The next day, Judy told Larry what he had done. She said he wasn't really happy, but laughed about it anyway.

CHAPTER SIX
A New Hobby and Lifestyle

Joe Naegler said he and Larry mainly worked on their cars each day after work.

"We worked at two places," he said. "I worked at C&H Engineering and could hardly work on the cars there. For the most part, we did lots of our work at the car lot, and the car lot had a nice shop in back.

"We worked on two cars at the car lot that was D&A Motor Sales. There was another car lot, out on Scenic Avenue and we worked on a cars there, and we had a little shop over on East Trafficway, and we had another shop down on College and Scenic that was a lot bigger building, and eventually Larry moved in the early seventies over on West Kearney (Street), and he stayed in there for three or four years before he moved over on Commercial Street. "

Promotional photo of Larry Phillips.

Dennis Slane collection

HELPING LARRY SUCCEED

"We both had the same goals to win races," Joe said, "but I think probably just as much as anything, Larry had a good business head on him.

"I put the cars together, and we had strength as a team, and I always had faith in him as a driver, to succeed.

"I said, 'One of these days he'll get that all worked out. And when he does, those other guys are going to be in a hell of a lot of trouble.' And he did. But we tore up a lot of cars in the meantime, and wrecked a lot of times. But I had faith in him because I could see that he had lots of ambition and real drive and determination about him, that he could succeed."

LIFELONG FRIENDS

"I was with him all through Larry's life at some point or another," Joe said, "but not every day. I

Dan Mahoney collection

Larry Phillips with his Modified and Late Model cars at Bolivar Speedway in Bolivar, Missouri, in 1999.

always said I was his financial adviser. I helped him if he asked me to help with something, you know, (like) a business plan or which way to go on business. I gave him my opinion, and a lot of times I helped him with different things that came up.

"At the same time we did a lot of work on emissions and transmissions and carburetors at my shop, but I didn't go every day, and run his business, but if he thought an engine needed to be freshened up or something was wrong with it, we worked on equipment all the time.

"We were always close, but there was times when he ran his life and I ran my life, and I was there for him, and if I needed something he was there, too. I had a key to his shop and he had a key to mine. If I needed something for my race cars, I went over and got it and wrote it down, and if he needed something from me, he came and got it. Many times he'd bring over an engine that needed to be freshened, but we just worked back and forth. In our lives, things would come up and, if it was important enough. I'd hear about it.

"I would say overall that … what you saw is what you got," Joe said. "Most of the time, the more he raced the more he liked it. And the more he wanted to do it."

"He'd stay pretty intense. That was the only way he could stay at the front," Joe said. "You couldn't be successful unless you were very serious, like Larry was."

Larry also has a caring side, Joe said.

"When I was in my forties I had my daughter, Nicky Joe, and she was just a little baby girl at the time, and I went over to Larry's shop to get something, and Larry sat there in a chair and held her for about three hours. He loved kids.

"He was a charitable person. And the people he cared about at Christmas time, and holidays he liked to have around, but he probably wasn't the same person at the race track that people saw," Joe said. "He had a softer side to him as he got a little older, and had a little more time and a little more success. And I'd say that the biggest thing about him was that he liked kids, and I think that he leveled some and got to where he found some other things in life that had value to him other than just going to the race track."

Larry Phillips driving his No. 4 car in competition during the 1970s.

Dan Mahoney collection

BIG-TIME RACER

"In our time, he was the big-time racer. And when we got into racing, the International Motor Car Association (IMCA), the United States Auto Club (USAC) and the Auto Racing Club of America (ARCA) were the big circuits," Joe said. "NASCAR was in the South. But they really weren't that big. … They had a few big races that they ran a lot of half-mile dirt [tracks], three-eighth mile asphalt track, and they had a few speedway races like Charlotte, Daytona and Atlanta. But other than that, most of the races were in half-mile dirt and a few asphalt tracks with guys like Ernie Derr (of Keokuk, Iowa, who won three-hundred twenty-eight Late Model races from 1951 to 1971) and Ramo Stott, who competed in USAC's stock car division, finishing second in 1973, 1976, 1977, first in 1975, and third in 1974 and was on the pole for the 1976 Daytona 500. But those guys were always the circuit racers, they ran IMCA and they ran USAC. And they ran ARCA. And our goal early in the sixties was to get good enough to run on those circuits."

"Then in the seventies we got good enough where we could outrun those guys. We could beat Ernie Durr, we could beat Ramo Stott. We could go down South and run against Bobby Allison, Neil Bonnett, Red Farmer (the NASCAR National Late Model Sportsman champion for three consecutive years from 1969 to 1971) and Donnie Allison or Pete Hamilton or Jody Ridley or even the great Darrell

Dan Mahoney collection

Larry Phillips drives his No. 75 dirt car on asphalt at the Craig Road Speedway in Las Vegas in 1979.

Waltrip. We went down there and competed with those people and drove for points.

"We were in Jackson, Mississippi, in '73 and Bobby Allison was down there and I was told Pete Hamilton was the big racer, and Jody Ridley was a big short track racer in the Southeast.

"We said we were thinking about going down and probably start running some NASCAR races, and Bobby Allison said, 'I don't know why you'd want to do that. You're making more money where you're racing than what we are down here.' And we were having some pretty good years back then," Joe said.

PRIZE MONEY
Joe said the prize money could sometimes amount to a lot of money; while other times, not.

"At times, there was fifty-thousand to seventy-thousand dollars in prize money. Then you had your sponsors and we had car sponsors and we had spark plug sponsors, shock sponsors—lots of things you used on your car. He said driving a race car has always been expensive," Joe said.

"Normally, a car with no sponsors would cost you fifty-thousand dollars to run if you were supported with power deals. Sometimes we even got free fuel, free oil, free transmission oil, free shocks and spark plugs and spark plug wires and batteries. We could run the car on twenty-thousand dollars because we built everything ourselves. We were buying very little parts, what I'd call store-bought. Everything was fabricated in our shops, so that was about how it played out. Most everybody that raced didn't just race and that wasn't their only income. Larry had his shop where he was building chassis and selling race car chassis parts, and I had my shop when I was working on street cars. But most everybody, even Bobby Allison, had his shops. He sold parts for his short track cars; he built short track cars there to help sponsor his NAS-CAR racing."

> "We could run the car on twenty-thousand dollars because we built everything ourselves. We were buying very little parts, what I'd call store-bought. Everything was fabricated in our shops, so that was about how it played out."
>
> —**Joe Naegler, Larry Phillips' crew member and best friend**

"It doesn't seem like it, but you could build a pretty good car from the ground up for five-thousand dollars with no labor involved," he said. "It's always a constant change, but, anyway, you always needed a lot of money to race. And I don't know if we ever went to a race that we thought what we had was good enough. We didn't want to waste money. But you always think you need more power, you needed a better handling car. And we never thought we had enough money. Larry may have thought there at the end, that his car was very competitive. And he had reached a point in the later parts of his career with the rules that he probably had the best equipment. But he'd tell you that there was probably something else he could do better. I don't think that he'd ever tell you that it was a good as it would ever get."

LARRY AND NASCAR

"Larry told me that he was out there at Ontario (California) and he ran down a corner and was pulling out a little loose," Joe said. "He didn't crash but he slid for a quarter of a mile, he said. When he was gathering it up, it wasn't completely sideways, and he said while he was doing all this Richard Petty and David Pearson went by. He said those guys were in a constant slide all day long. They didn't seem to mind it at all. But he didn't like it."

"He just didn't like the feeling," Joe said. "The car he was driving didn't feel as good as those guys' cars, but they didn't have any aerodynamics until they weighed four-thousand pounds or better. They went out of control, and if you look back at pictures of some of those cars, sometimes they were pretty loose. But he said those guys were all over the steering wheel and going on, and he was in his slide when they went by. He just didn't like it. Instead, he yearned for the short tracks.

Bill & Loretta Williams collection

"The Swagger"—Larry Phillips waves to the crowd prior to race.

And that's where he headed.

"Ray Pryor was probably the only one that ever beat us; he was a hell of a short track racer. He was very competitive; he beat us a time or two. But for the most part, wherever we went all over the South—we raced in Macon, Georgia, had a big half mile; we raced all over Georgia. Those guys never beat us. Wherever we went in the South, to Louisiana and we won down there. We went to Montgomery and went to Texas and we won there. It didn't make any difference. When those guys showed up—we'd just beat 'em."

NO FEAR

Joe is among many people who credit Larry with helping other drivers succeed in NASCAR, including Mark Martin and Rusty Wallace.

"Well, I think what they got from Larry was a big work ethic and a commitment to 'if you want to win, you have to work at it.' You just can't show up at the track and get in the car and drop the green flag, and you're gonna win the race. And what they learned from Larry was that it had to be totally prepared when you showed up at the track. You don't have much time, and you'd better be right when they drop the green flag. No time to make adjustments after that. I think, for the most part, what they got from Larry was they followed him a lot. But they had to learn quite a bit about running in traffic. More than anything, I think it was just if they could run with him or beat him some; it gave them a pretty big boost in confidence. But Larry was hard to beat, and those guys had to work hard if they did beat him. They were committed to their sport, and I think Larry had a lot of good technique. He could find holes and ways to get around you. If he ever got out, he'd be gone. Just racing with somebody that's real good makes you better, if you have any ability at all."

LOTS OF TRAVELING

"We never got back to run the Carolinas or Virginia, but we were all over Florida, Georgia, Mississippi, Louisiana and Tennessee," Joe said. "We raced in southern Tennessee, Colorado, California, Nevada, and New Mexico. Larry went all over the place and to British Columbia. We went up to the Dakotas. We raced as far north as Minot, North Dakota; Pierpont, South Dakota; Fargo,

Larry Phillips exits the old mail bus he drove to races in the early days. He carried equipment, and even his car, in the bus.

Judy Phillips collection

North Dakota; Minnesota; Wisconsin; Illinois; Iowa; Michigan; Indiana; Kentucky; Ohio; Pennsylvania—there aren't many states we didn't race in.

"When I look back on all of this, I used to think that sometimes we didn't do much, but it's a lot of work and a lot of commitment, a lot of time and traveling getting to where you want to get, but still it's a commitment," Joe said. "But when I look back on what we did, we did quite a lot. Those other guys did the same thing, not too many, but some; but most guys couldn't stand the pressure. It's a lot of work."

UNBEATABLE RECORD

"I don't think anyone will ever beat Larry's five national championships. That took a lot of commitment and a lot of extra effort. That is hard to do," Joe said. "But I think the other thing about Larry was that he was still getting it done. Some of those guys slowed down and quit, but Larry still kept at it.

"He just didn't do it all on asphalt and he was a versatile driver, and made his personal commitment to what he was doing. His work ethic probably what gave him some acclaim and acknowledgment from his peers was his commitment to what he was doing, but I don't think, for the most part, that a lot of these guys, or maybe some of them, in NASCAR, had that level of commitment. I don't see it. I think some of those guys have got pretty good talent. Their cars handle good; I don't know if they know if they are good racers or not.

Joe said Larry Phillips was definitely the master of the short track.

NUMBER 75

Larry's fans have often wondered how he happened to pick number 75 for his car. Although several tales have surfaced, Larry once explained it to Dan Engler, who published the answer in a feature he wrote.

"Several years ago, when I was getting started, there were only so many numbers available," Larry said. "I wanted number 25."

But there was one problem: "I couldn't afford a sign painter, so I set out

Larry Phillips said he actually wanted the No. 25, but couldn't afford a painter and drawing No. 75 was easier. Larry made sure to promote each of his sponsors every time he visited a track.

to do it myself," he said. "I never could paint a '2'. The '7' was easier and '75' was available. So that's what I've had ever since."

Larry reportedly enjoyed hearing the different explanations and said he fueled some of the rumors himself.

"Sometimes, just for fun, He would tell someone it means that he wasn't going to quit racing until he was seventy-five years old," Joe said.

TODAY'S COMPARISONS

Joe said, of today's slate of NASCAR stars, there are only a couple he would compare to Larry.

"Well, Tony Stewart is just one of those guys that can put on show anytime, and if it was a good car, he'd probably be up front when the night's over." Joe said. "He's pretty damn good, too.

"And Carl Edwards is probably in the same boat. I watched him race up at Lebanon a couple

Larry Phillips (wearing cap) with Bob Deeter, who taught him how to fly a helicopter and became a close friend.

of years ago and he's a hell of a shoot. That guy is a racer.

"Well, if Stewart wasn't really good as a driver, he probably wouldn't be around long, but the only thing that keeps him around is he's a winner. Larry … liked people and he liked to talk to them, but they'd wear on him if they got silly."

LARRY, THE AVIATOR
"Aviation was just another one of those things I think he just evolved into in the middle seventies," Joe said. "Larry got it in his head he wanted to fly, and he started taking lessons in 1974 and got his pilot's license, and he flew for maybe a year to a year and a half, and then quit. When he was flying, we were racing together then, and he didn't have to worry about getting the cars to the race track and he had more personal time, so he learned to fly. Then he'd fly to the races, and sometimes I'd fly with him to the races, and I'd take his car to the race tracks, and I'd come home with him, and someone else would bring the equipment back, but he liked it. Then I got to flying in the early nineties and he got back when I started flying. It wasn't long until he went and bought him an airplane again and got back into it."

"He got airplanes first. Then he decided he wanted to get a helicopter. But Larry really enjoyed flying, and he was a good pilot. He had good skills and he caught right on. Helicopters are a lot harder to fly than airplanes, and Larry got right onto that," Joe said. "I flew with him and he

Larry Phillips, left, and Rusty Wallace at the Ozarks Area Racing Association banquet in Springfield, Missouri.

Dennis Slane collection

was a very competent pilot. I guess I probably flew with him to see that Ernie Durr in maybe 2002 for his eightieth birthday, and I think that was probably the last trip that Larry made."

BOB DEETER
Bob Deeter is the flight instructor who taught Larry how to fly. He said he remembers the day that Larry first called him in 1995 asking about taking lessons.

Bob said he answered the phone and heard: "My name is Larry Phillips I understand you know how to fly helicopters." Bob said he told Larry that, while it was true that he flew helicopters, he didn't have access to one to use as a trainer. Larry said he would call Bob back. Four hours later, Larry called back and said, "I bought a helicopter, when do we start?"

Bob met up with Larry and started the training. It was the beginning of a great friendship. "Larry had a lot of friends," Bob said, "but when Larry called you his friend, he was true, loyal, dedicated and gentlemen, just a great person to call your friend."

Bob, who flies seven days straight and then has seven days off, was never a big race fan but said he was impressed by all of Larry's knowledge.

"He did not have a formal education, but he was nothing short of a genius." Bob said.

One day, Bob asked Larry "If everyone has the same engine, how one can be any better than the other one? Over the years Larry had studied engineering. He told Bob about cylinder wall thickness and minute details to make the engine perform better. Bob said he realized that Larry was not your average guy; he put his whole life into racing.

"Larry told me one day, 'These national championships, they don't give them away you have to take it.'"

Bob taught Larry to fly and said he expected him to fly "wild" in aviation. "We call that a 'cowboy,'" Bob said.

However Bob said his concerns were unfounded. He said that Larry was very professional and wanted to learn about flying the right way.

"We would be out flying and when it came time for lunch, he knew everyone everywhere so we would fly to the restaurants and people would see the helicopter out there; it was a real traffic stopper."

One day Larry told Bob that he wanted to review the rules of aviation "right of way" again. The rules govern powered aircraft versus non-powered aircraft (i.e. hot air balloons, etc). Bob asked Larry, "So what is your question?"

"Well there was a guy with a pick up turning left ..."

Larry Phillips takes a smoke break before a race.

Bob & Loretta Williams collection

"A pickup truck?" Bob interjected. "Where were you? Larry grinned and said, 'I was at the Battlefield Mall.'"

"When Larry wanted to do something, he did it," Bob said. "We had such a good time while we were training. Larry had never flown a helicopter and getting the hang of it with your feet and hands going in different directions, your head and eyes going in different directions can be overwhelming and stressful. "Sometimes we had to set the helicopter down because we were laughing so hard that we could not fly. We had a blast."

"Larry had more personal courage and spirit then anyone he has ever known and it really showed near the end," Bob said. "I can't imagine a stronger fight. He got out on motorcycles and did what he wanted to do right to the end. He was tough and they don't come any tougher than Larry Phillips."

ERNIE DERR

"He's another guy who was a hell of a good racer," Joe Naegler said. "Ernie Derr, for the most part, was the benchmark that most people set their sight on. Pretty much if you could outrun Ernie Derr, you could just about go anywhere you wanted to and win. He was a class act.

"He was a heck of a competitor. He went to Larry's funeral, and he respected Larry a lot. But we thought he was a more successful racer than we were because he was on the circuit and factory backed. But we got to where we could beat him. We got to where we could run with him. But he won thirteen IMCA national championships that were anywhere from one-hundred to five-hundred lap events. He always had factory backing, and he had good cars, and he was an old driver.

"For years, we didn't have enough car to beat him, but Ernie was a hell of a racer. Larry said he was one of the best he ever saw in his life. Ernie was his own good mechanic on his cars and we learned a lot from him. He respected Larry and we respected Ernie."

LARRY GOES BIG TIME

"I think he went to California on a short track, one of those short track tours, and he won everything out there, and he went back out there and did it again. He got a proposal to drive a NASCAR car in NASCAR events on the West Coast. They had good cars and good equipment, and they got him hooked up with Goodyear when he was out there. Then Larry got quite a few cars for asphalt through that deal. But they saw him on the short track. That's how he got in that deal."

RUSTY'S RIDE

Some people credit Larry with helping get Rusty Wallace a ride in NASCAR, but Joe says that's not exactly true.

"What I know for sure is that Rusty, when he first started his own, brought his own car to Springfield about 1978, he was just barely competitive. I mean, he was competitive, but he wasn't a winner.

Joe said Rusty went on tour and spent time on the West Coast.

"And I think what Rusty got out of it, he saw a style and a technique and, for the most part, I think Rusty imitated Larry."

Joe said Rusty's success came from winning on short tracks and then winning on the ASA circuit, making him a household name around the Midwest.

"A guy had a tire business up there, and he took an interest in Rusty, and he had a friend

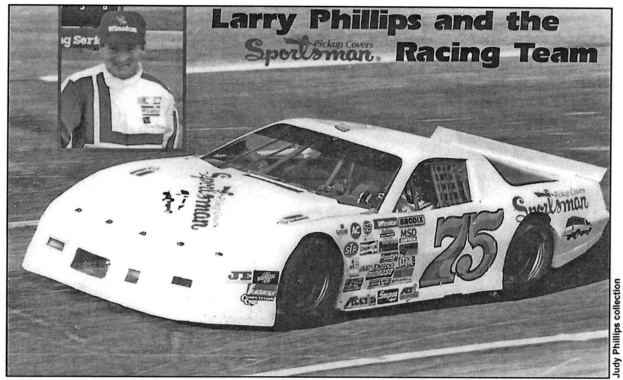

One of Larry Phillips' promotional photos.

that's with Penske, and they gave Rusty an opportunity to drive a Penske car at Atlanta. And that's how Rusty basically gained recognition.

"He hooked up with that Raymond Beal, a drag racer, and that's how he got going in NASCAR.

"Larry had a big impact on Rusty's early driving career," Joe said. "I don't know that, later on when Rusty got over in NASCAR, everything that Rusty learned racing with Larry had been used to enhance his racing abilities. But later on Rusty learned how to sit out there and run all day on the big track and not tear his equipment up and [how to] run into a problem and not wreck. He also learned how to go on and take the car and keep the tires under it and make it last for four-hundred miles, you know, keep the car together. But he learned a lot from Larry, there's no doubt about it. He'll tell you that."

Bob & Loretta Williams collection

Larry Phillips takes time for a smoke before a race.

CHAPTER SEVEN
The Sixties

Joe Naegler said he could easily recall Larry's later years and what mattered most to Larry during those years.

"I don't know if I gave you a good enough description about the early years. By the time we were twenty four, we'd only won one championship. And the next year, we ran on the IMCA (International Motor Contest Association) and we were always in the Midwest. We went on Friday or Saturday night specials with cars built by Chrysler Corporation. We got into pretty sophisticated equipment pretty quick and we learned enough about running on those circuits and running better cars from '66 on. I know one time in '68 Larry was running in St. Louis and he won a lot of money there.

"We took a car up there, I think it was our number 75 car, an Impala, but anyway, the race was protested. Larry won on that, and that did pay big money. It went to seven-hundred or eight-hundred dollars every week up there or better. A twenty-five lap feature in a heat race gets the better part of a thousand dollars.

"It was a little old bull ring, wasn't even hardly a quarter of a mile, and Larry just could

> "I guess you'd say we got so much better than the competitors, the end of '65 and on we were pretty well running over most everybody on the short tracks all through the countryside at twenty-four years old. So we had a lot of experience."
>
> **—Joe Naegler, former Larry Phillips crew member**

slay 'em up there and take their money. They said we were professionals," he said. "I guess you'd say we got so much better than the competitors, by the end of '65 and on we were pretty well running over most everybody on the short tracks all through the countryside at twenty-four years old. So we had a lot of experience.

"In 1962, they used to have some races at Joplin, (Missouri). They had a big modified field down there—quarter-mile dirt—and people came from all over that part of the country to race there and to watch them.

"We went down there to run stock cars against the modifieds, and we got about two-thirds of the way down there—this was on a Tuesday night—and it rained 'em out. And we were with

Larry's dad and decided, if we got turned around, we could get to Humansville (Missouri) and run at Humansville Speedway," Joe said.

"So we drove like hell and got back to Springfield, and at that time on these little highways with the little lips on the shoulders, they weren't very wide. But we got to Humansville just in time to get in the heat race. We unhooked the car and the tow bar and changed the right front tire. Larry jumped in the car, got in line and went down the straightaway. When they went through one or two turns, somebody put Larry across the infield, and he hit a big old pole, a good-sized pole like a telephone pole. He hit that thing dead center like it had a laser on it. It just bent the car to the ground," Joe said.

"I said to Larry when he got out of the car, 'Who was that son of a bitch that hit you?' and he said, 'I don't know.' It was a driver named David Goldsberry (the 1984 United States Auto Club (USAC) champion). So we drug the car back home and it was destroyed, and Larry went about building a new car in a week."

"They got the car done, but they didn't have any tow bars so we decided to tow it out to Fairgrounds (Speedway) on a chain," Joe said. "They made a fast run across town and they turned

Dennis Slane collection

A young Rusty Wallace kneels by his car for a photo at the Fairgrounds Speedway in Springfield, Missouri.

Dan Mahoney collection

Larry Phillips headed for another feature win at I-44 Speedway in Lebanon, Missouri.

the corner to go out there. And whoever was driving the stock car put some slack in the chain, and it got underneath the tire when they turned the corner, and it turned the car over. I can't remember who was with Larry, but … they turned the stock car back over and put it back on the chain and pulled it to the racetrack and raced it. It was from Campbell and Mount Vernon on out to Fairgrounds (Speedway). You know, how the hell they did that I don't know, but I'm sure he was exasperated at that point.

"I'm sure it wasn't too funny at the time, but probably later on probably everybody had a good laugh about it. There were many a car towed back then with a chain to the racetrack. There weren't any fancy car carriers or anything, no trailers. Most people used a tow bar, but that was a long time ago.

"Some people even drove the car to the race track," Joe said

OTHER INCOME
"We worked hard and made our race money off of our shops," Joe said.

"Larry used to tell the story that I sometimes didn't realize the impression I made on people. He'd always tell the story of how we'd go to Nichols [Auto Salvage] and go through the blocks and the crates and pick out our parts. We'd bring them back home and put 'em together so we'd have

Dan Mahoney collection

Larry Phillips, in foreground, battles for position during a race at I-44 Speedway in Lebanon, Missouri.

an engine. I just didn't think any other way; that's the only way we could do it.

"It made an impact on Larry's mind, because I heard him tell that story a lot of times about the sacrifices we made. He'd drive five-hundred miles to buy some used parts to build an engine so we could get in an IMCA race. We'd drive a thousand miles on a weekend to get some engine parts, and come back and go up after the race on Friday night and be up there on Saturday morning—drive all night to get those parts on Saturday—and drive back home, sleep a little on Sunday and go back to work on Monday. We'd get some parts to put together that week and then get an engine together and put it in a car and be somewhere that next week racing.

"In the early days, Larry liked to sleep a lot and work late at night. But as he got older, his work habits changed. He didn't care much about running his shop or running a business. He'd work if he had to, but when race time came, he was ready to work on the cars. He'd put in twenty-hour days if he needed to get done what he wanted to get done. But he would only bring a few guys who could focus and shut everything out, and whatever he was doing, that's all that mattered."

Dennis Slane collection

Larry Phillips racing at the Fairgrounds Speedway in Springfield, Missouri in the mid-1970s.

Joe said, during the summer, it wasn't unusual to catch Larry in his shop in the middle of the night.

"For some reason, there was something in it, and you don't find that in too many people who wanted to win. We wanted to win, and we loved racing, and we didn't care what it took, we just wanted to win. But, you know, we were pretty hard on each other at times. When he crashed in a race, I'd be pretty irritated at him sometimes for a day or two. Sometimes he'd get irritated at me for being irritated at him, and times we'd go at it pretty hard, but all in all we cared a lot about each other—and that binds people together."

"There was something that both of us needed from each other, that gave us both energy to handle the deal," Joe said. "I don't know what puts people together and how two guys from not really the same basic background, but somewhat similar, get started off on life and for both of us, there were things we had in common."

CONSTANTLY CHANGING
"Everything is involved in some sort of evolution that changes things," Joe said. "That's just the

way it is. But I'm fortunate to have a good life, and we made it ourselves. I've told people that many times.

"Other people told us we were very independent. But we got up and did what we wanted to do every day, in our own time and with our own money. And we'd drive off into the sunset and if we decided to run in the IMCA races at St. Paul, we got the car ready and went. You know, we always had the money some way. I didn't have any miracles, I'd say. But we decided we were going to do it, and we planned out things and we always had the money to do what we wanted. We never had to bounce any checks or worry about paying anybody."

> *"He didn't have a car he could win in. That's one thing that bothered him because he knew that car wouldn't win."*
> —**Judy Phillips, wife of NASCAR Winston Racing Series driver Larry Phillips**

In 1976, Larry was offered a chance to move up to the Winston Cup Series and on Nov. 21, 1976, he gave it a shot, racing in the *Los Angeles Times* 500 at the Ontario Motor Speedway in Ontario, California, in front of a crowd of forty-four thousand, seven-hundred two. Larry's earnings for that day were one-thousand, nine-hundred ninety dollars.

He drove car number 55, a Ford sponsored by Haddicks Towing, and his car owner was Jerry Lankford. Larry started twenty-fourth in a forty-car field and finished thirteenth after race leader David Pearson, who had the pole, won the race, earning two-thousand, seven-hundred fifteen dollars.

Other racers that day included Bennie Parsons, Dick Brooks, Terry Bivens, Cale Yarborough, Richard Petty, Donnie Allison, Darrell Waltrip.

Jerry was a car owner from 1973 to 1977. Sonny Easley was his driver during most of those years. Sonny tallied nine Winston West victories over his career, including a victory in the first stock car race ever held at the Laguna Seca Raceway road course. He finished second in Winston West points on two different occasions, in 1973 and 1975. During practice for a NASCAR modified sportsman race at Riverside on January 15, 1978, Sonny was killed when his 1968 Camaro slid across the track into a trailer and pickup truck near pit road.

But Larry knew the Winston Cup wasn't where he wanted to be. He told friends he'd rather be a big fish in a small pond than a small fish in a big pond.

And, Judy Phillips said, there was something else bothering him.

"He didn't have a car that he could win in," she said. "That's one thing that bothered him because he knew that car wouldn't win."

Larry quickly became frustrated with himself. He worried that his services as a driver would be sold to another team.

"That's when he told them to call Rusty (Wallace)," she said.

One of Larry Phillips' early cars was the No. 55 Haddick's Truck Parts car.

Larry Phillips headed for a feature win at the Fairgrounds Speedway in Springfield, Missouri.

Larry Phillips admires a Charles Schultz "Snoopy" poster with a caption that reads: "It doesn't matter if you win or lose—until you lose!" Larry had the same philosophy throughout his life.

CHAPTER EIGHT
Tragedy at Fort Smith

Larry spent a lot of time on the road traveling to tracks around the country. In doing so, he began building a national following. Everywhere he went, fans followed.

But Larry's dream almost ended in a fiery wreck about six hours south of his beloved hometown of Springfield.

On May 27, 1978, he was severely burned in a wreck while driving at the Tri-State Speedway in Fort Smith, Arkansas.

The wreck happened during the feature race and involved drivers D.J. Busby, Glen Hurt and Terry Deatherage, according to published reports. A fuel tank on one of the cars apparently ruptured, spilling flaming gasoline on the other vehicles.

One of Larry's crew members said Larry's Plexiglas windshield melted from the heat and dripped onto his hands. Larry jumped from the still rolling Chevrolet Camaro, but the flames and other damage left it beyond repair. By the time fellow racer Rusty Wallace got to his side, Larry's goggles had melted.

> *"Larry spent a month in the hospital at Fort Smith. It was third-degree burns and it took several months to recover."*
> **—Judy Phillips, wife of NASCAR Winston Racing Series driver Larry Phillips**

Terry Deatherage, of Wichita, Kansas, was sent to a Kansas City hospital, also with burns. According to published reports, he was still recovering from serious burns he suffered in the previous season from an explosion at his Wichita shop.

Bobby Menzie was competing that night and said he will never forget that night.

As Bobby came through the field, all the cars suddenly stopped on the track.

"Larry and another driver were racing for position and crashed," he said. "The car exploded into flames. It sounded like a bomb went off."

He said flames shot thirty feet into the air.

"The car was a ball of fire," he said. Everyone feared the worst."

Bobby said the scene quickly became chaotic.

Larry Phillips' car after a wreck at the Tri-State Motor Speedway in Fort Smith, Arkansas, on May 27, 1978. Larry suffered third-degree burns on his hands and some feared that he'd never race again. Four months later, he was again back at the wheel.

"There was panic and chaos both in the stands and on the track. Everyone was on their feet and women in the stands were screaming."

Bobby said that as the rescue crews were running to the scene both Larry and the other drivers struggled to get out of their burning cars.

"The heat was intense," he said, his voice growing quiet as he recalled the horror. "Larry wasn't wearing any gloves and when the car started burning the windshield melted over his hands. The shield on his helmet melted on to part of his face."

Bobby said that the only way he knew it was Larry's car is that he recognized the rear end, "the blue racer"—all of the other parts of the car were on fire.

Bobby said he was both elated and horrified by what he saw next.

"Larry rolled out of the car pretty quickly with his hands on fire," Bobby said. "He started to roll all over the ground, struggling to get the fire out."

Bobby said Larry later told him that the pain was excruciating but even more so when he rolled in the dirt in an attempt to extinguish the flames.

"There were fire extinguishers everywhere," Bobby said. "The car was toast."

Bobby said that Larry's helmet and visor was distorted from the overwhelming heat from the wreck. He said Larry tried to return eight weeks later at the Bolivar track. Following an eighth-place finish, Larry admitted he needed more time to heal.

Bobby said the experience taught Larry—and other drivers—a valuable lesson: One thing that Larry learned is that he should always wear gloves, and he did from that day forward.

News of the wreck and fire quickly spread throughout the racing community and fans from throughout the Midwest sought to learn Larry's condition.

The Springfield Daily News (now *Springfield Daily News-Leader*) reported on Tuesday, May 31, 1978, that Larry was in Sparks Hospital in Fort Smith being treated for his burns.

"A hospital spokesman said Phillips suffered third-degree burns, primarily to his hands," the paper reported. Doctors estimated a recovery period of about ten weeks, but the unnamed crew member told the newspaper he expected Larry to be racing sooner than that.

"Larry spent a month in the hospital in Fort Smith," Judy said. She said Larry then flew to Springfield, where skin grafts were done. "It was third-degree (burns) and it took several months to recover."

Some people doubted Larry would ever race again. But they didn't know Larry Phillips. After realizing eight weeks was too soon, Larry made a full return about four months after the wreck. And his determination to win grew even stronger.

"He was determined and strictly business at the race track," said Dale Roper, a longtime friend and fellow racer. Roper was track champion at Bolivar in 2002, the final year before it went to a dirt surface. He won seven track championships in a forty-four year career, two at Bolivar, four at Lebanon I-44 Speedway and one at the old Waynesville Speedway.

"Larry once told me he never felt he had to win every race, but he was afraid to lose one," he said.

"He always wore the Simpson fire suit and gloves after that," Dale said. "He was a pretty tough old boy."

Larry had been burned before, Joe Naegler said.

"The fire at Fort Smith hurt him physically pretty bad, but that wasn't the first time he'd gotten in a fire," Joe said. "He got in a fire in '65 in a car he built, a '57 Chevy with a guy named Don Swearingin, and they didn't even put any firewall in it, and it caught on fire and burned his leg and his hand some, and he drove at Fairgrounds Speedway with shorts on because his legs were burnt so bad he couldn't stand to have any jeans on the blisters. But we never missed a race, and in fact we won our first season championship. But he suffered quite a bit through that, but the burns he got in Arkansas did his hands in pretty bad. He thought for a while he didn't have enough strength in his hands to hold on to the steering wheel, but his hands did get better.

"He probably didn't do much for four or five months or maybe a little longer, and then he came back and got a car ready to go to California, and then he went to a big race down in Muskogee, Oklahoma, on dirt, and he stopped there and ran that, but it took him a while to get back up and get competitive again."

Bob & Loretta Williams collection

Larry Phillips returned four months after a fiery crash looking determined as ever.

Larry Phillips with Loretta Williams, trophy queen at the Fairgrounds Speedway in Springfield, Missouri.

Larry Phillips' car in front of the Goodyear Tire truck.

This promotional shot during the mid-1970s shows Larry Phillips with his House of Sound-sponsored car.

Photos from the Bob & Loretta Williams collection

Dan Mahoney collection

Larry Phillips poses beside his No. 75 car at Bolivar Speedway USA in Bolivar, Missouri.

CHAPTER NINE
Friends, Competitors Reflect

Bob Nelson is a former flagman at Fairgrounds Speedway in Springfield. Lester Friebe and Earnie Watson were fellow racers. The trio, who are all members of the Ozarks Area Racing Association's Hall of Fame, talked at length about their experiences with Larry.

"Larry was another A.J. Foyt—he did it his way," Earnie said. "In 1969, the first race of the season (at Bolivar Speedway), Larry came up to us and said, 'Boys, get out your crying towel; you're going to need it.' But my partner and I had the fastest time. We had a car called the Creepy Crawler we were driving that night. It was probably my best night of racing. It was always a great honor to get around Larry Phillips. If you outran him, you did it from behind."

Lester said he remembered many times Larry tried out new adjustments on his race car by driving on city streets.

"It would be ten o'clock or later at night," Lester said. "He'd get that car out on Campbell Street. It wouldn't be long before the police were out there. I don't know if they ever caught him or not. But he'd sure get out there and try that car out."

Lester grew quiet as he thought back to the early years.

"So many of those people are gone now," he said. "Larry, to me, was one of the most ferocious drivers I've ever raced against. He never apologized, but, in his own way, he'd make up for it if he thought he did you wrong."

Bob said Larry was responsible for him becoming a flagman.

"Bill Crockett had been the flagman at Fairgrounds Speedway for a long time—and he was good," Bob said. "When he died of a heart attack, they tried several different flagmen but none of them worked out.

"Larry asked me to consider doing it," Bob said. "I told him I wasn't interested. Then he talked with Bob Brown, the promoter, and told him they should talk with me. Bob called, Willie Crain and few more drivers called, and I finally said okay.

"Bob said he found that he enjoyed flagging and was told he did a pretty good job. Soon he was being asked to flag races in other parts of the country.

"I wasn't intimidated by someone ten laps ahead and letting them go," he said.

He said some flagmen will get intimidated and won't enforce the rules, causing the race to be delayed.

NASCAR collection

From left, Raymond Hammer, Larry Phillips and James Ince at I-70 Speedway in Odessa, Missouri.

"Sometimes it would be after midnight before the race would end," he said. "I went in and laid the law down where we could put on a two-hour show from eight to ten p.m. and everybody go home."

Bob said Larry didn't always like the rules and would often stretch them to the limit.

"The biggest thing that drew the crowds was Larry would show up late intentionally," he said. "He'd pretend to have car trouble or would change a tire.

"Larry knew he could come out and beat them. If he came out last he'd catch them in a few laps and pass them to win. The crowd loved it."

Bob said Larry got extremely upset with him during a race in Mississippi.

"It was a MASCAR (Mid-America Stock Car Racing Association) sanctioned race—the Pepsi 200 at Jackson International Speedway, a one-mile track. We had a lot of big names racing that night. Ned Jarrett, Wendell Scott, Marty Robbins, Jody Ridley, Dick Trickle—there were a lot of big names there that night," he said. "And Larry was just an unknown kid from Springfield. He was a nobody."

Bob said Larry surprised everyone by pulling away from the pack.

He said, as the race was winding down, a track official noticed some debris on the track in Turn Four.

"I couldn't see it from the flag stand," Bob said. "But the pitster said it was there so I stopped

Dennis Slane collection

Larry Phillips at the Fairgrounds Speedway in Springfield, Missouri.

Bob & Loretta Williams collection

Larry Phillips on the backstretch at the Fairgrounds Speedway in Springfield, Missouri.

the race so we could clear the track."

Bob said Larry was livid.

"He accused me of stopping the race to tighten up the field to make it a more exciting race," Bob said.

Larry eventually won the race, but he was still upset with Bob about the incident.

"Several months later, back in Springfield, I was having the drivers' meeting before the race, and I warned Larry that if he didn't come out for the parade laps I'd black-flag him. He nodded but pretty much ignored me," he said.

"Well, we had the parade laps and then started the race. Two or three laps later there came Larry and I black-flagged him. The crowd went ballistic. About half of the crowd was for Larry and the other half hated him."

But instead of heading to the pits, Larry decided to do something different.

"He pulled crossways on the track on the front straightaway," Bob said. "I decided to leave the green flag out."

Bob said he saw the rest of the field entering Turn Three and knew he only had a few seconds to decide whether to stop the race to keep Larry from getting hit.

"Then I realized his car was still running," Bob said. "But the cars were into Turn Four and there were only a couple of seconds before they'd be all over Larry."

Bob said he decided to call Larry's bluff.

"It didn't take him long when he saw the forty-five tons of cars coming at him. He went through the infield and came out on the other side driving in the wrong direction around the track. The other cars continued racing."

Bob said, when Larry got to the flag stand, he climbed out of his car and removed his helmet.

"He stood on the track right under the flag stand and shook his fist up at me. I ignored him."

A few laps later, a wreck on another part of the track caused the race to be halted.

"I climbed down from the flag stand and Larry was there."

Bob said each man called the other a bad name and they cursed the other before turning and walking away. The tension lasted for a while. But, eventually, the men moved on and became good friends.

And Bob said that friendship continued to grow as the years went by.

Bob said he holds one distinction in his experiences with Larry.

"I was the only flagman to black flag him (at Fairgrounds Speedway)," Bob said.

Earnie said he also had fun with Larry.

He made a T-shirt with the saying "Larry, you think I'll ever be as good as you are?" "I had a banner made and out of Larry's mouth I put, 'No.'"

Dale Roper raced from 1965 to 2002 at Fairgrounds Speedway.

Larry started racing about 1960," Dale said. "He started getting good about 1966 or '67. When he first started, he was like everyone else.

Dale remembered Larry's first championship.

Above, track officials survey the situation to see how best to right Larry Phillips' car after he flipped it during a race at I-44 Speedway in Lebanon, Missouri. Larry came back to win the race. Below, Larry Phillips, left, helps his crew right the car.

Photos from the Dan Mahoney collection

Dan Mahoney collection

Larry Phillips, No. 75, takes the lead at a California track in the '70s, followed by NASCAR great Ernie Irvan, driving No. 10.

"When he saw he was getting close to winning, he brought in a pavement car. I was running a modified. He called me and told me he had bought a second car. Back then NASCAR had a rule that you couldn't bring a spare car to the track. He called and asked if I would drive his car. I started at the back since I didn't have any Late Model points.

He came on the radio and asked, 'How are you doing back there?' I said, 'I'm doing okay."

Dale said the next time he heard from Larry, he was running in third place and closing in quickly on Larry .

"Larry came on the radio and asked, 'Is that you Dale?' I told him it was and he said, 'That's far enough.'"

Dale said Larry tried to be patient with his fans but sometimes, his patience ran out.

"Larry once told me he couldn't figure it out. He said, 'Somebody will shove a one- or

Here's another Larry Phillips promotional photo with his popular No. 75 car.

two-year-old kid up wearing an old dirty diaper and a T-shirt and you can see where you signed the same shirt last year.'"

And once a lady came up to him after a race and asked if he had any T-shirts.

"He looked at her and said, 'What do I look like, Wal-Mart?'"

A West Coast driver, Rick Sharp, said Larry was also particular about the money he won.

He said when Larry started driving in California, he'd put his winnings in a shoe box. He said if Larry had a large sum of money, he'd sleep with it.

He said winners at tracks in the Midwest and East Coast usually only won a thousand dollars at the most.

Terry Brumley was another racer who worked for Larry for a time.

Terry was only a few years younger than Larry, but he looked up to his older friend.

"When I was a kid, I used to go to his shop and try to pick up pointers," Terry said. "Later, we were both racers and, like everyone else, I wanted to beat him."

Terry said after many attempts, it finally happened.

"I happened to beat him one night at Rolla Speedway," he said. "And Larry called me the following Monday and asked me to go to work for him. I ended up working for him from late 1969 until 1978."

Terry said he felt a kindred spirit with Larry.

Dan Mahoney collection

Larry Phillips in his Kelley Radiator Service-sponsored car.

"He was like an older brother to me," he said.

He said when leaving wasn't an easy decision. But family obligations came first and Larry couldn't offer benefits such as medical insurance. Still, Terry helped out when he could.

"I'm a welder," he said. "I'd make spindles and other things for him."

Terry, who said he later built Rusty Wallace's first car at Larry's shop, said Larry was focused on winning and was "very competitive."

"He's a no BS kind of guy," Terry said. "He called things like he saw them."

He said there's one trait he admired most in Larry: Determination.

"He didn't have much more than a high school education," Terry said. "Everything he knew, he taught himself. Larry played hard but he worked harder."

Terry said Larry's son, Terry Gene, started coming to the shop when he was just a child.

"He must have been six or seven years old," Terry said, "Larry was gone a lot back then so me and a guy named Mike Edwards took Terry Gene with us to ride motorcycles and we'd take him over to see motorcycle races."

He said Terry Gene didn't express a desire to race until he was older—and Larry didn't push him to race.

"He started out racing go-carts," Terry said. "Later on, Larry helped him get a modified (car). Then Larry got him a late model (car). Larry raced on pavement while Terry raced on dirt."

Larry Phillips takes a few hot laps at the Fairgrounds Speedway in Springfield, Missouri.

Terry said two big names in NASCAR remind him of Larry.

"Oh he was an early Dale Earnhardt in my opinion," Terry said. "And today, he's Tony Stewart all the way."

Terry said it was almost like losing a member of the family when Larry died.

"When we lost him, it almost killed me."

JAMES CHISM

James Chism was another one of Larry's longtime friends and a fellow racer.

"Larry and I talked several times about the championships, things he'd been through," James said. "We talked about the Winston Invitational in Florida. Anything that paid money he was right into. And this national championship sponsored by Winston at the time, was one of the all-time greats. It brought pride to all of us, the pride that we were running against one of the top individuals in racing. And we had an option to go for one-hundred fifty thousand to one-hundred sixty thousand doolars in prize money every year, plus the regional and the local money.

"We were proud of what we did," James said. "We had a tough field of cars. You race against the best, you are the best. But we all wanted to see somebody from our track win that national championship because it brings more pride to you than anything you've ever done."

Judy Phillips collection

NASCAR President Bill France, left, presents Larry and Judy Phillips their championship rings at the 1991 NASCAR Winston Racing Series banquet in Nashville, Tennessee.

LOOKING FOR MORE

"Larry was out after another championship," James said. "There wasn't a doubt in anybody's mind. I loved it. You know it made us all feel good and here we are back again.

"This time we found that we're in a West Coast Region, and the only way to make up another race is for us to drive to California on a weekend to do it, and there's no doubt in my mind or anybody else's mind why this had happened. It was to stop Larry from winning another championship.

"Well, surprisingly, that didn't work either. He kept going just like he always had. He kept winning just like he always did. There was no thing too big. Larry was one of the hot rods in racing. Hot rod and knew how to handle it. He was good.

"We even got split up," James said. "We got in several different divisions in the Winston Racing Series. We split up all over the place. It was hard to make any of the races but what the heck. If you get rained out of one, you go to another one.

"I don't believe that anyone believed any higher about himself as Larry did. It became a fight between him fighting the system. The same system he always fought as a kid. I admired him for it; I admired him for everything he did.

"Larry was much more than a winner," James said. "It was the Winston Invitational … Jeff

Larry Phillips takes another feature win at I-44 Speedway in Lebanon, Missouri.

Purvis would drive his car all week long during the other races and Larry would step in for the Invitational. He'd run as hard as he could. He's won several of them. He told me he lost one time because he didn't see the white flag come out. Mike Eddie beat him and, you know, he was really uptight about it.

"We were sitting in his shop one day, Bobby Blunt—Bobby Blout, as they called him the Indiana Outlaw, myself and Larry, and a few others, talking about some of the things that was going on and, you know, it's tough to be an individual that understands and wants to do better, but he wants to go on with his life. Larry just wanted to keep succeeding.

"We were on a trip one time and he said, 'Jim, you know I get the same question all the time: How come I didn't go big time? How come I didn't go big time?' And to me it was hard to understand because, in my eyes, he was big time. I mean, you put him on a track with any driver in the United States, you put him on that short track, and he's going to beat them. I saw him and Jim Weber, who is another one of my heroes.

"Jim Weber was tough, the toughest in the business. Him and Larry had a match race at Lebanon—ah man—and Jim Weber would not give … He was another Larry Phillips. He wouldn't give to anybody. Neither did Larry. They didn't run them, they'd win them.

"They ran two races. Weber won the first one and Larry won the second one. They didn't run a third one because everybody knew there would be no cars left for the feature if they did because they were going to destroy each other. They had too much will to win. I have been very lucky to get to see some of the people that I've seen over my lifetime. The race against Eddie Hoffman, Steve Carlson, Brian Hoop, Kevin Cywinski, you name it, man, superstars of the world short track business. It felt like running Daytona, Talladega, you don't have time to put your arms up on the post and rails. Every second, you got one, two, corner; one, two, corner; one, two, corner ... You don't have time to rest. You're always in action; you're always moving; you're always working at it. It wears you out quick.

Five national championships is something that might never be broken by anyone—thanks to noted NASCAR crew chief James Ince, Bart Bates and people like them. They helped Larry win those championships, but it was up to that man in that number 75 car to do it all.

FIRST MEETING
"I remember when Larry first started racing on a dirt track at the Fairgrounds Speedway, and he was always the showman," James Ince said. "He'd make it to the races about five minutes before they started and never got any practice laps in. Everybody always waited to see whether Larry was going to show or not. That was the big thing.

"Larry understood things about racing that a lot of people will never know. He devoted his whole life to it. It was his passion."

"Larry is a very sensitive person, very caring. Most people never get to see that. He's a different person when he hits the racetrack. You know the thousands and thousands of stories we've talked about, being gone for days at a time, it was worth every second I was gone away from home to just get to hear these stories from my hero, and a guy that did become my best friend."

THE BEGINNING
"Larry told me when he first started out racing in St. Louis, they were laughing at him," James said. "[They] laughed at his car, laughed at him, laughed at the way he drove. The funny thing was, about four weeks later, he said, they weren't laughing anymore. Instead, they were trying to figure out what he was doing to beat them.

"And that's how he came to know Bill Schrader (Ken Schrader's father), and the stories just went on and on and on from there. And you know, these people that Larry helped out along in life like Mark [Martin], Kenny Schrader, Rusty Wallace and everyone else, they've all tried to do something to show their respect for the man that did help them.

"Larry threw the Duke Stoddard book at me one time. I'll never forget, he told me, 'When you know this you'll know the basics of setup. My gosh, have you ever seen the book? It's about three inches thick, mostly algebra, geometry and calculus. And, if you know it, you could completely design all the geometry on a race car from the ground up.

"It's very complex. I did, I read the book probably about fifteen times, I've seen the tapes about thirty times, and I understand about ten percent of it at this point."

EXPANDING HIS HORIZONS

Larry was fast becoming a racer to be reckoned with. Other drivers knew if the number 75 pulled into the track, it was going to be one more great night of racing. And Larry continued making a name for himself as he reigned in win after win.

One of the drivers Larry came to know was a man who had already established himself as a fan favorite: Carlisle, Arkansas' Tommy Joe Pauschert.

Tommy Joe already had several titles under his belt, and he wasn't impressed by Larry just because of his name. But he said the drivers each learned to respect the other early on.

Tommy Joe said he remembers that first meeting.

"I met Larry when we were both racing in the National Dirt Racing Association," he said. "(Larry) was a very dedicated person when it came to racing. He wasn't a very likable person back then. But he was dedicated racer."

And it didn't take long before the two drivers found themselves at the front challenging for the win.

"One time at Bolivar (Missouri), he bumped me and [at] the next corner I spun him out and he went over the end," Tommy Joe said. "It was a funny thing because ever since then, me and Larry always raced together, and we could race each other clean. I never had a problem with Larry after that.

"After that race we talked," he said. "[Larry] was from Missouri, and it seemed like everybody in Missouri was sort of scared of him, and I told him, "I

Larry Phillips smiles and waves to the crowd following another win.

Dan Mahoney collection

don't know what your deal is, but I have nothing against you. I have nothing but respect for you as a racer. But you're not going to take me out because, if you do, I'm going to take you out."

Tommy Joe said the two became friends after that.

Bob & Loretta Williams collection

Larry Phillips' "Blue Racer Camaro" parked behind his shop on Commercial Street in Springfield, Missouri.

"I think Larry had respect for me racing—as much as Larry could have. But you have to remember that he could be a very difficult person back then. Not to take anything away from his racing at all. I'm saying he was just that serious about racing. We raced a lot in the NDRA together and traveled a lot together and became closer friends as time went on.

"Well, we were as good of friends as you could be with Larry while he was a racer. Larry was two different people. When I knew Larry as a racer he was one person. And then the last four years, Larry went with me to, I guess, every motorcycle event I went to. He was a completely different person—day and night difference."

Tommy Joe said every driver who ever competed against Larry learned a tremendous amount from him.

"Larry had a hand in making racing better for everyone," he said. "He made me a better racer, too. Because when you raced against him you had to be a better racer. He gave one-hundred ten percent every time he went to the racetrack. You didn't beat Larry Phillips giving a hundred percent; it took a lot more than that."

Judy Phillips said Larry enjoyed the days of riding motorcycles with Tommy Joe Pauschert. She said the two of them often cut up having fun. But one time, that fun almost got Larry arrested.

"Tommy Joe and Larry went to Daytona on their motorcycles," she said. "They were at a stop sign and Tommy Joe made it through the stop sign and Larry didn't. So Larry sat there revving his engine waiting on the light to change. When the light changed Larry, not knowing there was an unmarked police car behind him, started to spin his tires, and filled the policy car with smoke, sand and gravel. After he went through the stop light the policeman pulled him over and wanted to take him to jail. Instead Larry got a ticket and had to go to driving school. He was mad at the time, but when he looked back on it he just laughed about it."

A RACER'S RACER

"James Ince (who later became Larry's crew chief) was telling me one time that when he first went down to Jack Roush's Busch Team for Mark Martin and they were setting the bump steer with toolboxes and Larry was far advanced on that," said James Chism, a former competitor. "He had been doing things like that for years ahead of his time. That's why he started winning races. He wanted to win bad enough he started looking for every aspect that it took to make that car faster on that racetrack."

"Not only his driving style made him faster, but his cars made him faster. There is one point that he had over everyone else: being able to read the race car, know what changes to make, and make those changes that would affect you toward the end of the feature race—and that's the only one that counts. If you don't cross the line, then you have no paycheck; you've done nothing. The last lap is the only one that counts in a race. And Larry learned how to be up front on that last lap every night almost.

"And the starts were remarkable," James said. "I've been behind him hundreds of times. You look up on a start and he's gone. You don't even know where he went.

"One of Larry's new fashions had been motorcycles," James said. "I ran into him one night at the Adobe Restaurant, and he wanted me to ride with him, behind him. 'No way, José!' I said. I've seen this movie before; he's as crazy as I am. I would have loved to, but then in a way I thought I'd found a

James Ince, a member of Larry Phillips' crew, at the NASCAR Winston Racing Series banquet in Nashville, Tennessee, on November 1, 1996.

Judy Phillips collection

Dan Mahoney collection

Larry Phillips driving his dirt car on pavement at Craig Road Speedway in Las Vegas, Nevada, in 1979.

new life so I really didn't want to kill myself right off the bat.

"He enjoyed it. He enjoyed everything that he did from airplanes to motorcycles, to racing. Everything was a passion with him," James said.

"I never have regretted a second of time that I spent with that gentleman. The championships he went through, all five of them, he had to work for very hard. The man had to win almost every race. He couldn't mess up. He hated not to finish. But he had to race as hard as he could and win them, and that field of cars was not one that was easy to overtake. They had all become as professional as he had; they were just as tough. There were a lot of the new rookies sitting out there wanting to take his place. Jamie McMurray, Timmy Swearingin—a lot of people wanted to beat Larry Phillips.

"When you're on top of the world, everybody wants you. I, myself, I wanted it, too, but I wanted him to have the championship.

"One of the last things I ever did with Larry was the Kyle Petty Charity Ride," James said. "We were at the Chateau on the Lake at Table Rock Lake. It's a good memory."

Bobby Menzie, who grew up as one of Larry Phillips' biggest fans, is one of many drivers who credit Larry's influence with giving them the courage and opportunity to race.

BOBBY MENZIE

Bobby Menzie, a longtime friend and fellow racer, said he and Larry first met when Bobby was perhaps eight or nine years old. Larry's dad, Jim Phillips, owned the Phillips Speed shop and Racing Equipment on College Street, and Bobby's mother worked at a restaurant nearby. Larry often came in for lunch. Bobby's mother and Larry's dad also knew each other.

Larry's dad also owned several rental properties and Bobby often mowed lawns for him. Later, after Bobby started racing, Jim told him, "You're wasting your time Bobby. You can't outrun Larry. That's all he does for a living. All he thinks about is racing and you can't beat him."

As Bobby got older, Larry became a good friend and mentor. Bobby bought several chassis from Larry and painted Larry's cars. Larry built both dirt and asphalt cars so Bobby estimated that he painted more than one hundred cars for his racing idol.

Bobby said Larry was the kind of person who thought that if you worked for him you had to think like he thought. For example, Bobby said he was picking up parts one day and had a boy

Bob & Loretta Williams collection

Larry Phillips poses with his good friends and fans, Bob and Jane Smith.

working for him. Larry was aggravated at the boy.

"If I pick up a chisel, you better pick up a hammer and hand it to me," he told the kid. He wanted anyone who worked for him to think like he did so he could work more efficiently in the shop. Larry didn't like wasting time. Bobby said if you were around Larry, you better be dedicated to racing and getting the cars ready. "Larry thought about racing twenty-four hours a day," Bobby said.

Bobby said Larry was also quite a character at the track. He said he once went to Larry's pit to ask Larry if he could borrow a set of quick-change gears. "[Larry] said, 'Yeah, I will loan them to you, but if you have any kind of trouble with your rear end I want to know about it because you could cost me a win or ten-thousand dollars.' He was very particular with who he loaned his parts to for that reason."

> *"Larry understood how hard it was to race with an injury and he wanted to make sure the car was right to avoid any more injuries."*
> —**Bobby Menzie, fellow driver**

Bobby competed against Larry quite a bit but could never beat him. Bobby said he thought he had Larry beat once at Airport Speedway in Springfield when the race came down to the white flag lap. Bobby said the drivers were side-by-side heading for the finish line. Suddenly, "Larry edged me out by about a half a fender," Bobby said.

Bobby raced for about twenty-five years and then helped his son Matt begin his own racing career. Larry helped Bobby set up his cars when he had trouble with them.

Bobby said Larry's racing insight was impressive. On one particular occasion, Larry got in Bobby's car and told him that the seat wasn't installed correctly. Larry told him that the seat needed to lean more to the left more so when he was in the corners he could see better.

He said that although Larry was a stiff competitor, he always did the best work he could do for any driver whose car he worked on.

In 1973, Bobby wrecked and broke his leg at Bolivar Speedway. After the wreck, Larry built Bobby a new car and did much of the welding on the car himself to make sure it was safe. Bobby said, "Larry understood how hard it was to race with an injury and wanted to make sure the car was right to avoid any more injuries."

Larry needed to go to Michigan after the races at Lebanon I-44 Speedway one night and asked Matt if he wanted to come along. Matt told Bobby that he carried a notebook around and all along the way, he wrote down ideas about racing as they came to him.

Bobby said Larry was intense when it came to racing, but he could also be hilarious and loved to play practical jokes. He said Larry had a trick that he often pulled on the guy riding in the front seat with him. If Larry was driving, he would be riding along and Larry would close his right eye and the passenger would think he was asleep while he was driving but his other eye was open and it would scare everybody.

Dan Mahoney collection

Larry Phillips waves hello to his fans.

As a kid, Bobby said he often went to the Fairgrounds Speedway in Springfield and watched Larry race. One night Larry kept jumping the starts and Bob Nelson, the flagman, warned Larry about it. Basically, the rest of the field could not keep up with him at the starts, so Bob black-flagged Larry. Larry stopped the car on the track. There was a wall on the front stretch and the officials' booth was at the top of the stands. He said Larry jumped over the wall and walked all the way up the steps to a walkway where the officials' area was. Larry got to a wooden gate and it was locked so Larry kicked the gate off of the hinges so he could talk with the officials. On the way, he passed Bobby in the stands. Bobby said that, as a child, having Larry walk past was a memorable experience. "As a young kid you're sitting right there and [it was as if] God just walked by you." The black flag remained.

Bobby said Larry had several quirks; one of them being that he never wore a shoulder strap tight. "He wore them loose and got into a wreck in Rolla. It broke his sternum and collar bone and then he wouldn't ride in an ambulance because he did not want to make a big deal out of his injury. Someone took him in a station wagon and drove him back to Springfield to the doctor. Larry wanted to be tough and ready to race no matter what the circumstance were. He was the 'Dale Earnhardt,' the 'John Wayne' of racing," Bobby said, "He wanted to have you mentally beat before the green flag ever dropped." Bobby said that Larry once told him that several racers had cars that could outrun him, but mentally in their minds, they could not beat Larry Phillips.

When he was a child Bobby often rode to Larry's father's speed shop on his bicycle. "Anytime kids would come around, Jim would run them off but I had front row access," Bobby said. He said that Jim did not generally like kids in the shop.

Bobby said Larry had rules at the shop that everyone had to adhere to—no matter who they were. He said he was at Larry's shop one day, and he had a guy coming in from out of state who had a chassis that Larry built that was wrecked.

"This man also planned to buy a motor from Larry. He was going to spend quite a bit of money—maybe twenty-thousand or thirty-thousand dollars. They unloaded the car and pretty soon they pulled out a cooler of beer in his shop and opened the cooler. Larry immediately went over to the guy and slammed the lid shut on the cooler and said to put it back in the truck. There was no beer allowed in his shop. Larry never drank beer while he was working on his car."

Bobby said Larry often couldn't get anything done during the day because so many people constantly came in to buy parts. So Larry started working on his own cars in the afternoon. When anyone went to Larry's shop to get parts, they had to wait for him to finish whatever he was working on at the time.

"That's the way it was, if you were smart at all," Bobby said.

Bobby recalled an incident that happened once at the Fairgrounds Speedway that made quite an impression when he and Larry were racing on asphalt. Bobby drove a '69 Nova that Larry originally built and said he went down too hard in Turn One and spun. He said Larry pulled up beside him. "You know, you're down there with God in Turn One and God is coming over to you and he looked in my window and said, 'What in the hell were you thinking?' I replied, "I *wasn't* thinking."

Rusty Wallace sometimes raced there, too. He built his own chassis and Kirn Racing Engines built the motors. Larry started helping Rusty and gave him his first Howe car and chassis; that's when Rusty started to be a contender, Bobby said. Bobby said Larry once told him that there was no one he had seen or was around that had more determination and more work ethic than Rusty Wallace. Rusty impressed Larry and that's why Larry wanted to help him.

"He saw the raw talent was there but the cars were not and that is where Larry stepped in,"

The engine compartment of Larry Phillips' 1977 Camaro.

Bobby said.

He said Larry had a way of putting people down often without them even realizing it. Bobby remembered one instance in particular: "A guy came to Larry's shop one time and said, 'I've got a son that is a heck of a driver and I want you to let him drive one of your house cars.' Larry replied, 'Yes, we can do that. I'll tell you what you do. You go back to your Realtor and sell your house and come back and bring me money from your house and your son can drive it.' Larry was very humorous and always had a line to come at you with."

Bobby said Larry was extremely proud that his son Terry became a racer. "Terry went out there to Manzanita Speedway in Phoenix, Arizona, a few years before Larry passed away and won a big race. Larry ran down the best he could to hug him and congratulate him much like when Dale Earnhardt congratulated Dale Jr. for his first win. It was very emotional."

CHAPTER TEN
Conforming to New Rules

In 1989, Larry was forty-seven when NASCAR sanctioned some of the tracks where he raced. So he joined the organization. But he soon found he had to make some adjustments. And Larry didn't like that.

Two tracks that converted from dirt to asphalt were Lebanon (Missouri) I-44 Speedway and Bolivar Speedway USA (Missouri), formerly called Bolivar Speedway. Both tracks were built and operated by Bill Willard, who owned Willard Quarries.

For more than two decades, Larry had been a successful Late Model driver. He traveled from track to track as a "bounty hunter," collecting extra winnings, or bounty, that promoters put on regular track winners. He did this without much structure from any sanctioning body at the time. He won many races—two thousand or more by some estimates—but he didn't get the recognition he surely deserved until he began driving in NASCAR-sanctioned races. And Larry wasn't sure he wanted to join the organization. But an old friend, Joe Kosiski, the 1986 NASCAR Weekly Racing Series National Champion and

National Dirt Late Model Hall of Famer, finally convinced him to give the organization a try.

Larry had lots of experience in racing on what were called pavement tracks. Some were asphalt while others were concrete. In the ten years prior to 1989, he made lots of money as a bounty-hunting, dirt Late Model driver. The most he ever won from chasing points was season-end award of one-thousand eight-hundred dollars.

While Larry's earnings increased because of the points fund awards, he hated having to abide by someone else's rules. He finally got some recognition and made his mark upon NASCAR for an entire decade, but he didn't like the banquets, ceremonies and other hoopla required of the champion.

Although he never completely changed, Larry adjusted and came to accept those responsibilities. After winning five national championships and seven regional titles, he became more comfortable with the fact that he was respected—and his fan base was expanding.

Judy Phillips said Larry put tremendous pressure on himself to win the Winston Racing Series Championship. She said winning it brought even more pressure.

"It was really hard on him," she said. "But I was tickled to death that he won it. And, you

Larry Phillips pauses for a photo at the Ozarks Area Racing Association banquet in Springfield, Missouri.

The 1996 Gatorade Champions gathered for a promotional photo. Pictured are, front row from left, Kelly Tanner, Lyndon Amick, Dave Dion and Joe Kosiski; second row, from left, Chris Raudman, Terry Labonte, Randy LaJoie and Tony Hirschman; back row, from left, Mike Cope, Ron Hornaday Jr., Lance Hooper and Larry Phillips.

know, it was his turn to take the stage, because he had won lots and lots of races."

"In 1989, the NASCAR banquet was held at Opryland in Nashville, Tennessee," Judy said. "The banquets were always held around Christmas time and the hotel was always decked out with poinsettias and Christmas decorations. Judy said, "Larry could not care less about the first banquet. He did not want to associate with anybody, he just wanted to get his money and get the hell out of there. Larry hated everything about the first banquet. He had to play golf with Darrell Waltrip and he hated it, and it was cold they almost froze to death. But as he won more championships and went to more banquets, he started to enjoy the banquets and playing golf with Darrell Waltrip.

"There was an official at the banquet who was trying to help Larry with his acceptance speech and Larry did not want any help, Judy said. "He told the woman he already knew what he was going say."

Dan Mahoney collection

Larry Phillips takes another feature win at I-44 Speedway in Lebanon, Missouri.

PAUL SCHAEFER

In an interview with NASCAR's Paul Schaefer a few years ago, Larry talked about the lack of media coverage of his racing during the early days.

"We've probably won six-hundred features and almost every major event there is to win in this part of the country, and the most attention we've ever gotten is a two-inch story in the newspaper," he said.

But he never sought the publicity.

"I am not a glory-seeker," he told Paul. "I don't wear a shiny uniform. I get dirty. I like to work on these things. But you do like to have pride in the fact that people know you, and when you go someplace, people talk to you and have respect for what you do. That makes you feel good."

One of the first congratulatory phone calls Larry received after winning the 1989 championship came from Joe Kosiski—the friend who originally convinced him to give NASCAR a try.

"I called him to congratulate him," Joe said at the time. "I told him he's never seen anything like what was going to happen to him at the banquet. He's one of only eight people in the world to wear that weekly series championship ring. We talked for about twenty minutes and I think he still didn't realize how big of a deal this really is."

Larry once explained his racing philosophy to Paul: "Coming from behind is actually an advantage for me because of my experience in all the years of racing," he said. "I should know by now how to get through traffic and how to anticipate what competitors are doing on the track.

"We study this thing. We don't just drive onto the track and when they throw the green flag, look up in the air and decide what we're going to do then. We look at the lineups. We watch each competitor in the heat races. How did each of them do last week? How are their cars handling tonight?

"Racing won't wait on you. You can't sit there and wait for them to hand you a big check. You've got to take it. We're not going to rough somebody up to win, and we don't go to races to beat this competitor or that competitor. We go to win. We may end up running last, but I think we can win every race we start."

As much as Larry learned to love winning races and the accolades that come with it, his favorite part was driving—most of the time.

"A good-handling fast race car, there's nothing like it," he told Schaefer. "A poor-handling race car is the worst thing you can have to deal with. If you're winning, it's fun. If you're not, it's not. It's that simple. There's a challenge each and every time you unload that car."

He produced an average of ten new cars a year.

"We try to help them whenever we can," Larry said of those who purchased cars from him. "We do something a little different in our business operations. I don't know how other people do things, but anything our race car team has is definitely available to our customers as well. If I can't win races on my ability, using the same equipment as our customers, then

I don't need to win. Our chassis business is a long-term deal. After I retire from driving, I hope to still have that business as a way to be involved in racing."

Larry hinted for the first time that he was looking ahead to the day when he would decide to stop.

He added that he probably wouldn't be a team owner, fielding cars for hired drivers. But his next statement left that door open.

"You can't say what you're going to do or not do. The right deal could come along and you'd be right back in business. We're definitely not ready to retire from driving, but things are changing. I have some other interests."

Those other interests included learning to fly.

Larry had taken up aviation as a hobby, and was flying county to county in his new Robinson R-22, a two-person helicopter. He received his helicopter pilot's license on December 26, 1994, and flew almost daily for the pleasure it brought him.

Judy said she and Larry often flew to restaurants.

"We'd fly down to Lambert's, (a restaurant in Ozark, Missouri) and land in the back of it," Judy said. "The owners came out and got us out of a line of people and took us to the front so we could get in and get out. And we would fly over to Johnnie Loos (a restaurant in Springfield that closed several years ago) and land behind his restaurant.

But Larry was not going "soft." At the age fifty-two, he was finally learning how to enjoy himself.

CHAPTER ELEVEN
A Second Title

In 1991, Larry wrote a new chapter in weekly racing history by becoming the first driver to win a second national championship. The season was also the tenth for NASCAR's weekly short track program.

With the new season came changes for both Larry and NASCAR.

NASCAR had a new method for computing points to determine a champion, and Larry opted to commute the long drive to two tracks in the Kansas City area—Lakeside and I-70 Speedway—that were added to the series that year. Larry also added a new two-man crew that year, twenty-two year-old James Ince and Raymond Hammer. James had been a farmer while Raymond had been helping Larry off and on for several years.

NASCAR introduced the Competition Performance Index (CPI) formula that year. The regional champions' records were formulated using the index and the regional winner with the greatest results won the national championship. The factors of the CPI equation included winning percentage, average number of cars in feature events, and the percentage of available races started.

Now fully familiar with NASCAR's weekly series, Larry worked hard to win a second title. In forty starts, he had thirty-two wins: fifteen at Lakeside Speedway; thirteen at an Odessa, Mo., track; and four wins at Lebanon.

He seemed to enjoy the fruits of this championship better than his first one.

"We tried much harder to win this championship this year than we did in 1989," Larry said at the time. "I'm getting close to the end of my career, and I may never have this opportunity again. I wanted to do it one more time in 1991. Winning the championship a second time in the series' tenth anniversary makes it even more special.

"We didn't worry about the points until the last six weeks. When it got down to the end, we had to run a fine line of not getting too over-confident or too under-confident."

Larry rarely spoke about feeling pressure, but after winning the title again, he admitted it wasn't easy.

"If anybody says being in the race for the [NASCAR Winston Weekly Racing Series] national championship isn't hard on their nerves, I wouldn't believe them," Larry said at the time. "Sure, I've been up in the middle of the night setting valves and rechecking things ... making sure things were right while it was quiet and the phone wasn't ringing. My normal workday is fourteen to sixteen hours a day anyway, mostly on the race car.

"This has been a tense season, but I'd rather be a racer and have tension than to be sitting home in an easy chair. Being a racer is all I ever wanted to be.

"The tension is strong, but I'm thankful to NASCAR and all of the sponsors who have given us and all the weekly racers the opportunity to compete for the championship."

NASCAR President Bill France presents a championship ring to Larry Phillips' wife, Judy, at the 1995 NASCAR Winston Racing Series banquet as Larry looks on.

Larry Phillips, left, with NASCAR Vice-President Jim Hunter at the 1989 NASCAR Winston Series Championship banquet in Nashville, Tennessee.

CHAPTER TWELVE
Another Year, Another Title

In 1992, Larry showed no signs of slowing down. In fact, his career hit its high-water mark that year capped by his third NASCAR Winston Weekly Racing Series championship that netted him sevety-seven thousand, seven-hundred fifty dollars.

On July 3 of that year, Larry celebrated his fiftieth birthday. And he didn't let age slow him down. He posted thirty-eight wins in forty starts that season.

He was undefeated for the entire season at his two primary tracks: Lakeside and Odessa. The two races he did not win were at Lebanon I-44 Speedway, the track closest to his Springfield home. One of those was a top-ten finish, making the season's tally forty starts, thirty-eight wins, thirty-eight top-five finishes and thirty-nine top-tens.

GAINING A SPONSOR

His success also spread beyond the track.

Fate smiled on Larry when someone asked Sportsman Pickup Covers owners Dale and Steve Brallier, a father and son team, if they would be interested in sponsoring a race car. They were given Larry's phone number and called him. Already familiar with short track racing, they discovered that their sponsorship brought brand recognition to their product. Larry and the Bralliers hit it off well and worked out a deal.

The first year, Sportsman Pickup Covers was strictly a sponsor. After that year, they became like family. Steve told Larry it was the "perfect marriage" and agreed to sponsor him for as long as he raced—and he did.

For the first time in Larry's thirty-three year career, he had a corporate sponsor. Larry was proud of the sponsorship.

During radio interviews, Larry often espoused the benefits and quality of Sportsman Pickup Covers. He knew how the product was made and its applications.

Steve said the sponsorship proved to be successful.

"It was better than a marriage relationship," he said. "Larry hated losing more than he loved winning."

And Larry proved it by capturing his third—and at the time his most savored—championship.

Larry Phillips made a national television appearance on "The Ralph Emery Show" in 1992. He is on the back row in the center.

"This was as close to a perfect season as we've ever had in my four years of NASCAR racing, as well as my whole career," he said. "We ran good race cars. The cars were well prepared, had no engine trouble, [I] missed the spins [by other drivers] and cut only five tires the whole year."

But the near-perfect season almost ended early in disaster for Larry.

On August 21 that year, Larry and his two-man crew, packed their new enclosed trailer and headed for the third-to-last NASCAR Winston Weekly Series points weekend at Lakeside Speedway in Kansas City, a two-hundred mile trek each way.

Larry had just completed a two-year project of restoring and renovating an enclosed trailer capable of carrying both of his Sportsman Pickup Covers Late Model cars and all of the equipment needed to maintain them.

"It was the first trip for this new rig and everything on it was brand new except for the rear tires," Larry said.

"We were about halfway to Lakeside going down a hill and one of the left rear tires blew out. The hauler wiggled and I started to slow down. As I did, the other tire blew out and then it really wiggled.

Larry Phillips, center, was one of the 1989 Gatorade Circle of Champions. To his left is Rusty Wallace.

Judy Phillips collection

"We got stopped right in front of someone's house, so we used their phone and called somebody who brought us two tires. That took an hour and I was starting to get nervous. After the new tires were on, I sent James on ahead to Lakeside in the other truck to get us registered to compete.

"We finally got going again and as I drove, I checked the mirror frequently to make sure there were no problems back there."

But a simple mistake almost cost him dearly. A small piece of rubber had somehow gotten lodged in the brake drum. And that small piece of rubber almost caused Larry to lose his cars, his hauler, and the championship.

"We'd gone about thirty miles up the road when I looked back and saw fire coming from under the left side of the trailer. There was a farm house about a quarter-mile up ahead so that's where I headed.

Larry and Judy Phillips at the NASCAR Winston Racing Series banquet in Nashville, Tennessee, on November 1, 1996.

"Just as we got there, the air lines burned through, the rear brakes locked up and twisted the drive line out. It stopped right there in the middle of the road.

"It was starting to burn pretty bad. I got the back door of the hauler down while [crew member] Raymond [Hammer] ran to the farm house to get hoses and a bucket. He started getting water on the fire while I went inside to get the cars out. There was so much smoke you couldn't see, and I was crawling around on the floor trying to get the cars unhooked to get them out of there.

"I was inside when a tire exploded and the whole thing felt like it jumped three feet. I got the first one out, and by the time I got the second one out, the fire department arrived. It took them about fifteen minutes to get it completely out. If they hadn't gotten there so fast we would have lost the whole truck. They did a tremendous job."

Reality quickly set in. What the fire didn't destroy, a missed race night at Lakeside would.

"There we stand near a farmhouse with no way of getting to the races, knowing the only double feature of the season [is] on the schedule," Larry said. "James is already at the race track getting ready to have a nervous breakdown because he doesn't know why we're late. I'm thinking that we could lose everything we had been working for if we miss these two races.

"Then someone told us about another person who had a roll-back truck he used to haul heavy equipment. We got a hold of him and he arrived in about forty-five minutes. We loaded a car and left everything else behind.

"The guy did a great job of getting us to the track. The truck only had two seats, and here I am sitting on Raymond's lap all the way. We made it to Lakeside just in time for our heat race, which we had to run to be eligible for the feature. We ran the heat race then won both features.

"It was pretty tense and hectic for a while," Larry said. "I wasn't hurt, but we could have lost all our equipment, the race cars, the hauler, and the championship."

It took two days to get everything back home to Springfield from the farmer's yard.

Over the two remaining weeks of the season, Larry continued to run out the season with wins at both Kansas City-area tracks.

The hauler fire incident demonstrated Larry's rare, instinctive courage. Despite the fact that he had been in a racing accident in the mid-1970s in which he was badly burned, Larry, with no visibility due to smoke, showed no fear in crawling around the floor inside his burning rig to un-chain his two race cars. His actions were, in his thought process, strictly common sense. The race cars were the tools of his trade. Without them, he could not work.

NASCAR collection

Larry Phillips, the 1989 Gatorade Champion.

CHAPTER THIRTEEN
Skipping Two Years

Although Larry didn't win the national championship in 1993 or '94, his record was still the envy of many drivers and fans.

In 1993, he won his third consecutive and fourth overall NASCAR Winston Weekly Racing Series regional championship. His racing record for the season was thirty starts, twenty-three wins, twenty-five top fives and twenty-top tens. Barry Beggarly of Pelham, North Carolina, won the national championship after the final race night of the season shoot out for the title with Dennis Setzer.

"My nerves have been much better this fall," Larry said. "I'm glad it's them and not me, because I know what they're going through."

He spoke as if he was actually looking forward to attending the series champion's banquet as a regional champion.

"Winning the region, I'll get to go to the banquet, wear a tux, and make a speech. Last year, the legs of my pants weren't the same," he said, laughing.

He had discovered one of the pant legs of his tuxedo was longer than the other when he was putting it on for his 1989 champions' banquet, which frazzled his nerves, because he wouldn't try it on until it was time to go. He also confessed that he had never worn a tuxedo until that night.

In 1994, Larry scored twenty-seven feature event wins—more than any other regional champion that year. David Rogers of Orlando, Florida, was the 1994 national champion. David made the mythical "dream season" a reality, winning twenty-two features in twenty-two starts to win the title.

Larry won his series-record fifth regional championship, surpassing the prior record of four held by the late Richie Evans (1982-1985). In owner records, Larry tied Iowa powerhouse owner Larry Eckrich (1987-1991) with five.

Larry's racing record for the season was thirty-five starts, twenty-seven wins, thirty top fives and thirty-two top tens.

After years of setting the standard in local competition, Larry realized the competitive level of his peers had been raised as well.

Judy Phillips collection

Dale Brallier, right, with son, Steve Brallier, at the NASCAR Winston Racing Series banquet in Nashville, Tennessee, on November 1, 1996. The Bralliers own Sportsman Pickup Covers, Larry Phillips' main sponsor.

"On certain nights, ten or eleven drivers could win," Larry said. "We build chassis, and some of these young drivers come to the track with them, so we indirectly make it harder on ourselves.

"Racing here locally has come a long way since we joined the series in 1989. There are a lot more fast cars, a lot more quality cars, and the competition is a lot closer."

David Roger's 1994 national championship got Larry's attention.

Another factor boosted Larry's focus. David was the first in series history to win the national title with awards exceeding one-hundred thousand dollars—one-hundred fifty-thousand to be exact.

The cash factor made the race shop behind his farmhouse an even more attractive place for Larry to spend his time during the long, cold Southwest Missouri winter in preparation for the 1995 season.

In 1995, Larry again raced at his local tracks at Lebanon and Bolivar. His crew then consisted of Bart Bates, Les Blizzard and Brandon Linnebur.

Things got interesting as the points added up and the weeks remaining wound down.

A young driver in Washington had captured Larry's attention as the season wore on. Greg Biffle, twenty-five, of Vancouver, Washington, was racing Late Models at Portland (Oregon) Speedway and Tri-City Raceway in West Richland, Washington. He had led Larry in the regional points race much of the season. Larry, now fifty-two, had to play catch-up in the regional points race. At the end of the season, the two were tied in points. It was evident that, based on their racing records, whoever won the region would become the national champion.

> *"Our main competitor, but not our only competitor, was Greg Biffle. I've never met the young man, but evidently, he's a heck of a racer."*
> **—Larry Phillips talking about future NASCAR driver Greg Biffle**

Larry won the championship, worth one-hundred thousand, six-hundred fifty dollars, in a tiebreaker, the highest number of feature wins. Both drivers had impressive records for the season. Larry: Forty starts, thirty-two wins, thirty-eight top fives, and thirty-nine top tens. Biffle: Forty-three starts, twenty-seven wins, thirty-four top fives and thirty-seven top tens.

"Our main competitor, but not our only competitor, was Greg Biffle," Larry said, following the race. "I've never met the young man, but evidently he's a heck of a racer. Each driver has to do the best he can in every race. That's what we've done, and I'm sure that is what he's done.

"We had our challenges this year, mainly from our fellow competitors here at Bolivar and Lebanon. It wasn't just Greg. The cars and drivers here are more competitive than ever. Their cars are faster and there are a lot of newer guys coming up. They've got a lot of talent.

"This year, Mike Goldsberry started off slow, but in the second half of the season he became a real factor. Paul Wallen and Robert Webster are tough. Robert won three features this year and each time he just flat outran us.

"Everybody else is moving forward in their racing programs while I don't seem to be advancing much."

Larry estimated that about fifty percent of "everybody else" was driving race cars he had built.

Dan Mahoney collection

Trophy queen Summer Perry poses with Larry Phillips after a win.

CHAPTER FOURTEEN
Back to Business

Larry's 1996 national championship wasn't his easiest, but everything fell into place just at the right moment.

In the end, he pocketed thirty-six thousand dollars from the Heartland Region Point Fund Award and seventy-eight thousand dollars from the NASCAR Winston Racing Series National Championship Point Fund Awards, giving him one-hundred fourteen thousand dollars for the season.

He had a rough start to the season and weather threatened its completion. His winning percentage for the year dipped, and at the halfway mark of the season he was third in the national rankings. He also experimented by fielding a single car instead of his typical two (one for each track), testing the theory of racing "hard" (two cars) versus racing "smart" (one car).

If one car came home in bad shape from the track, only Larry's son, Terry, also an accomplished dirt Late Model racer, and one crewman were scheduled to help on a limited basis. There was hired help, although Larry's shop drew frequent visitors and friends who also pitched in.

Dennis Huth, NASCAR's vice-president of corporate communications, lauded Larry's accomplishment in announcing the winning of another championship on November 1, 1996, at the Opryland Hotel in Nashville, Tenn.

"Larry Phillips has achieved greatness in the NASCAR Winston Racing Series, just as Richard Petty and Dale Earnhardt have in NASCAR Winston Cup Racing," he said. "And he continues to add his legendary stature with each passing season. Dynasties are a major part of sports history. The Boston Celtics, New York Yankees, Montreal Canadiens and UCLA Bruins are forever a part of the legends of sports because of the greatness they achieved. Larry Phillips has become a dynasty in the NASCAR Winston Racing Series. "

Observers picked up on that and soon started tossing the word "dynasty" around in conversations surrounding Larry's fifth NASCAR Winston Weekly Series national championship, but Larry was having none of that.

"The only dynasty I know about is that it's the name of an old TV show," Larry quipped. "We go into each season not trying to do anything more than win the next race. We're not counting points or trying to win titles, we just want to win races.

Judy Phillips collection

Larry and Judy Phillips with David and Joi Bates at the NASCAR Winston Racing Series banquet in Nashville, Tennessee, on November 1, 1996.

"We might take a look at the points about halfway through the season, and we're in decent shape, then the pressure might begin. After the last race of the year, I'll know I've done all I can do—and that's the best I can, one race at a time."

After beginning his NASCAR career in 1989, Larry scored two-hundred one feature race wins in two-hundred forty-eight starts, a career winning percentage of eighty-one percent.

Opening night of the season was a less than stellar beginning to what would prove to be a rewarding year.

"I got involved in two incidents on the first race night of the year at each track; I had to re-evaluate my driving abilities," he said, in a rare public expression of his sense of humor. "After that, things settled down, though."

Larry wasn't optimistic about his championship chances as the first half of the season progressed.

"I actually spent the first half of the season rooting for Carl Trimmer to win the national championship this year," he said. Trimmer was the longtime top driver at Tucson (Ariz.) Raceway Park.

"Carl's a good friend. I've talked to one of his crewmen, Frank Buckner, often during the season."

However, it wasn't Larry or Trimmer leading the national standings at the halfway point of the season. Mike VanSparrentak, a seasoned Late Model racing veteran at Kalamazoo (Michigan) Speedway was first in the nation at the season's midway point. Trimmer ranked second, followed by Larry.

The points race equation required twenty starts to be eligible for a regional or national championship, and weather played an important role for Larry's title bid. Despite a rainy weekend at Lebanon, Larry was able to pick up his nineteenth and twentieth starts, to have a chance at the titles. He also won the track's Lake Model division championship. He did not win the track title at Bolivar, however. Kansas City's Paul Wallen took those honors.

"I'd say I got lucky to win the national championship this year," Larry said. "I certainly am grateful to the people at NASCAR and Winston and all the series sponsors that make this type of program possible. My sponsors, Steve and Dale Brallier, and the whole bunch at Sportsman Pickup Covers have been with us for five years, and they've been great to work with."

When the regional champions' records were calculated through the CPI formula, Larry won the national championship by two one-hundredths of a percentage point over NASCAR Modified driver John Blewett III, who competed at Flemington (New Jersey) Speedway. Larry's racing record overall included twenty starts, fourteen wins, and eighteen top-ten finishes.

It would be as close as John would ever come to the title. On August 16, 2007, while competing in a Whelen Modified race at Thompson Speedway in Connecticut, he crashed and lost his life.

Despite the race wins, track titles, regional and national championships, Larry's peers were envious, but not jealous.

"Larry's been racing for about thirty-five years, and I think he's made all of us better drivers by setting a high standard," Paul Wallen, a fellow driver, said in an interview at the time. "Winning the track championship at Bolivar this year means more to me because Larry Phillips was on the race track."

Archie Griffin was also a close friend and competitive driver.

"It's no secret he does everything one-hundred percent," Archie said of his friend. "He's as tough as they come and a smart driver, but he's also a great friend."

Fellow driver Doug Anderson summed up Larry as perfectly as anyone ever had:

"Larry's been a lifelong friend. When it comes to racing, he knows just about everything there is to know, and he's still learning. He's an excellent fabricator. He can make a few small adjustments to a car and make a huge difference in it. When he's driving, he stays out of trouble by actually driving ahead of himself. He's consistent and his laps are perfect just about every time around. Usually he's the class of the field.

"Larry Phillips is just a natural born racer."

"In 1996, the very last year that we went to the banquet, they added on to the hotel and we stayed a long way from where we had to be and Larry always got lost trying to find his way back to where he was supposed to be. The drivers got together a lot at the banquets and Larry started to have a good time with Paul Schaefer as well and the drivers and the NASCAR officials.

"Larry did not want anybody to think he was stuck up or better than anyone else. He was proud of himself and proud of NASCAR. The drivers still played golf and Larry started to like hanging out with Darrell Waltrip."

CHAPTER FIFTEEN
More Accolades

Larry was inducted into several racing halls of fame, including the Missouri Sports Hall of Fame, Springfield Hall of Fame, the Ozarks Racing Hall of Fame and the National Dirt Late Model Hall of Fame.

Larry was inducted into the Missouri Sports Hall of Fame on April 11, 1996, and into the Springfield Hall of Fame on April 11, 1996. Others notables in the Missouri Sports Hall of Fame include Stan Musial, Rusty Wallace, Len Dawson, Payne Stewart, Marcus Allen, Tony LaRussa, Ozzie Smith and George Brett.

The Ozark Area Racers Association was formed in 1987. Its mission is to preserve the history, photos and memorabilia of stock car and oval racing in Southwest Missouri; to promote the history of racing and to gain recognition for the pioneers of the sport; to organize and conduct meetings or other promotional or educational activities and to organize and operate an annual "Ozarks Area Racers Reunion."

The group's hall of fame selection committee looks at the number of feature wins, the drivers at the Fairgrounds Speedway, and how long they've been racing.

They name inductees either "Legends" or "Pioneers." Legends are race car drivers. Pioneers are those who had an impact on racing.

Larry was inducted as a Legend in 2001.

Longtime motorsports journalist Bill Holder proposed creating The National Dirt Late Model Hall of Fame in 2001.

Its voting board consists of thirty car builders, media, promoters, sanctioning body heads and engine builders.

The board votes for five active drivers with at least fifteen years of experience, five major contributors to the sport and five drivers who are retired for the last five years.

The first class of inductees, which included Larry Phillips, was introduced at the annual North-South 100 at Florence Motor Speedway in Florence, South Carolina, in August 2001.
James Ince was Larry's crew chief for several years. James moved to Charlotte, North Carolina, a few years ago. Just recently, he spoke about his old friend.

"I probably first met Larry when I was three or four years old," James said. "He and my

Dennis Slane collection

NASCAR great Harry Gant, right, poses with Larry Phillips at the Ozarks Area Racers Association banquet in 2003.

dad were friends. They raced together at Fairgrounds Speedway and kind of grew up around each other."

"I believe I went to work for Larry in 1990. I was actually racing locally around there and kind of got upset with the racetrack and decided I wasn't going to race for a little bit. One day out of the blue Larry called me and asked if he could make a deal with me that if I came and helped him out he'd teach me everything I needed to know about racing. So it was an opportunity I just really couldn't turn down at the time. I actually just left myself parked and went to work for him.

James said he began working with Larry just as Larry was moving his shop from downtown to his farm in the country.

"Believe it or not, I ended up being the one that had to finish emptying the Commercial Street shop out." The former shop was later destroyed in a fire.

Larry Phillips' towing rig parked in front of his shop in Commercial Street in Springfield, Missouri, ready to go racing.

Bob & Loretta Williams collection

"I have a lot of memories out of that shop that I remember when I was a little kid going and visiting him. That's a hallowed piece of ground right there."

James said Larry taught him more than just racing.

"I don't know if it was specifically anything that he taught me on purpose. The reality of life is that Larry taught me how to race. He was a very, very hard person to work for and to be around. He was such a perfectionist that there was no loafing or getting away with anything with Larry. You actually had to give it everything you had every single day. You just couldn't be around Larry without learning things. He kept a lot of things close to his chest and wouldn't teach you a lot.

"But we spent a lot of time riding up and down the road and, as times went on, he just talked more and more, and we'd talk about the cars, and I think he was a little bit surprised that somebody of my age at that time, not necessarily knew so much, but was trying to learn a lot. I was never in a position that I just wanted to know; I wanted to make it work and I was willing to work hard.

"I never wanted to go to the racetrack and not win races," James said. "So, it was an odd situation that our personalities kind of meshed and the fact that we both had the same goals.

He said Larry talked about a lot of things, but somehow racing dominated the conversations.

"We talked about lots and lots and lots of things. And ninety percent of the time we would talk about racing and designing cars and what did what. But he also would kind of mentor me, and it was kind of a unique deal. I grew up with Larry being my hero and somehow he turned into my best friend.

"And you know, it wasn't always racing, maybe it was life instances" that were discussed, he said.

"I got married in 1992 for the first time, and he took me racing in Carson City, Nevada, and I believe ninety percent of his attention on that trip was to tell me that I was too young to get married and I didn't need to be married.

"He felt like I had a future in racing and, you know, he was just a mentoring guy all the way across the board. It's kind of hard for most people that ever knew Larry to think you could go to him and talk about something and get an honest answer, but you could.

"Most people knew him as somebody you couldn't take your troubles to," James said. "But I was always able to do that, and I was pretty young. I went to work for Larry when I was eighteen and he taught me a lot about life, and he for sure taught me everything about racing. He was a guy that I've looked up to my entire life, and he was my Richard Petty or Dale Earnhardt as they are to other people. Most people, if they ever went to the racetrack as a fan in the grandstand, would definitely have a different perception on how the guy really was."

James said Larry was so good in the 1970s that promoters in Springfield brought in other drivers to try to beat him. They brought in Donnie Allison once, and Larry beat him so soundly that Donnie said the devil couldn't beat Larry on that track.

"And there was this one time over at I-70 Speedway in Odessa—back when it was a dirt track," James said, "one of the race promoters announced he would give five-hundred dollars to anyone who could set the track record for a lap.

"Well, there was a hole in the middle of the race track that day, and the turns were slick as ice on a fender. [It] wasn't much of a day for setting records. But you have to understand there wasn't a thing Larry Phillips would not do in a race car when someone put five-hundred bucks on the line.

"So he shoved his left foot below the brake, jammed the gas to the floor and held on tight. He pushed his number 75 Chevy fast as it would go, soared over the hole, raced banzai through the turns, and hit the finish line with his hand sticking out of the window. He was reaching for the five-hundred bucks. He got it, too.

"When he got out of the car he was shaking. [That was] the only time I ever saw Larry Phillips scared. There wasn't anybody else on earth that could have made that run. Damndest thing I ever saw in a race car. I'd say of the ten most amazing things I ever saw done in a race car, Larry Phillips did nine of them."

James said Larry meant business when he raced. He raced not just for fun, but to win.

"I think a lot about it is desire and just the fact that second place wasn't acceptable with Larry

Larry Phillips with pit crew members Raymond Hammer, left, and James Ince, right.

and he was never allowed not to be the best. He was one of those rare bosses that if he disagreed with you, it wasn't a situation that you would get in an argument and he might withdraw, and to me that was a good thing.

"During the week (Larry's son) Terry and I prepared the cars and took care of the cars, and when we got to the racetrack we were ready to race," James said. "And there was no doubt that when the time came, you were strapped with the best guy in a race car that you'd ever possibly be lucky enough to work with.

"I recall that before we started on the second championship with Larry, the third, even, my dad told me that there was no way we could repeat," James said. "That was '92 and we won thirty-eight out of forty, a lot more races than the year before. We went to the racetrack with the mentality that we were not going to be beat.

"Now the other thing that people really wouldn't believe and understand at that period of time is that we also went to the racetrack with a different setup every single night. We were trying different things and doing different things and experimenting. And he wasn't a guy who was will-

Dennis Slane collection

"The White Knight," Dick Trickle, wins a feature race at the Fairgrounds Speedway in Springfield, Missouri.

ing to say, 'Okay, this is the setup you put the car in once every week.' We were constantly trying to get better. And I have never seen anybody that, even on the nights that the car wasn't right, he made it right. Larry was one of those guys that literally strapped a race car on. He didn't climb in it, he strapped it to his back and he went out there and he did what he needed to do to win.

"It's one thing to say it, but with him it was true: Larry was the first person I've ever been around in my life that would truly have rather died than finish second. He was going to do what needed to get done to win the race. And if we didn't have two flat tires that season it would have been a perfect season on the statistics. And it was just a lot of work and a lot of dedication. I don't think people realize that during that period of time we worked a minimum of twelve hours a day, seven days a week, and when we got to the track, we were ready to race.

"A lot of times we would get back home from racing at I-70 (Speedway in Kansas City) at four in the morning, and if he didn't make you come into the shop at noon, it was a rare opportunity. There were a few times when I was dirt racing with (Larry's son) Terry Gene on Sunday nights. But that's what we did twenty-four seven. It was all about going in and winning races and trying to win a championship."

BAD FOR BUSINESS?

"When Larry showed up, he was the guy to beat, and he was that way for years," James Ince said. "When we raced at Lakeside Speedway, we were always seeing rules being changed because he was so dominant in a race car. They would bring in ringers and they would pay guys to come in and beat you. A lot of things went on over the years that Larry was able to overcome and work through, and it bothered him. There was no doubt that it bothered him, but what are you going to do? When you're the big fish in the pond, everybody's out to get you in any way that they can get you. At the time, I believe, all the promoters viewed it as a fact that Larry winning every week was bad for them. If you look at the local listing now, you can see that it was good for them. Look at the car count. Bolivar and Lebanon still struggle with that today. So it's a Catch-22. And you can never hold it against the promoters what they were trying to do because they were trying to put on a show and make money. And it is tough when you've got somebody at this caliber that is stinking up your show every week.

"There was no doubt that Larry Phillips Southwest Missouri racing was the Dale Earnhardt or Elvis Presley. I mean, either you wanted to come to the racetrack to see him get beat, or you wanted to come to the racetrack to see him win; there was no gray area. So [promoters] were trying to keep themselves in business, and I don't think they really understood what they had there. At the end of his career, I think, him and Bill Willard kind of caught on a little bit and, thank God, would be easier to get along with. But that part of it was always a struggle. The political side of it was just never an easy situation.

"There was a situation at Lakeside in 1991 that they actually painted a line around the racetrack, and you could either run off the bottom or you could run off the top, and you got three warnings if you crossed the line, and after the third warning they disqualified you. Larry got a warning one single time, and they actually disqualified him that night. And it was a big deal because people didn't understand that's how I was making my paycheck. So situations like that never really surprise me because they would do anything so competitors couldn't gain. The racetrack themselves would do the best they could and make it happen.

TOO MANY TROPHIES

James Ince said the rumor that Larry regularly cleaned out his trophies is a fact.

"And I'm sure, looking back as he got older and retired, that was one of the things that he regretted," James said. "The man was at the racetrack for the paycheck; he didn't go for the trophies. Toward the end of his career he would give them to kids or fans in the grandstands. So I don't think most people realize that he's five-time national champion."

"But the majority of his races were won way before NASCAR ever came to Southwest Missouri, way before the pavement stuff ever happened. He traveled for twenty years before that all over the United States winning every big race there was. So there were a lot of trophies collected over the years."

Judy Phillips collection

Everyone was all smiles as Larry Phillips received his check for another NASCAR Winston Racing Series championship year as his wife, Judy, looked on.

A PROMOTER'S DREAM

Randy Mooneyham, promoter at both the Monet and Lebanon tracks, said Larry was to short tracks the same thing Dale Earnhardt was to the NASCAR Winston Cup Series.

"Even people who didn't like him were a fan of his," Randy said. "People either went to watch him win or they went to watch him lose. Either way, it was Larry Phillips they came to see.

"He was a fierce competitor," Randy said. "In my years of [promoting tracks] I never saw anyone work so hard on their race cars."

Steve Brallier, left, and his father, Dale Brallier, right, owners of Sportsman Pickup Covers, Larry Phillips' main sponsor, pose with Larry at the NASCAR Winston Racing Series banquet.

Randy said Larry first impressed him many years earlier.

"One of the first races I put on, I'm twenty-eight years old and here comes Larry Phillips. He was like the big dog coming to the track. As fierce as he was, he didn't believe in running second. If he got beat, he didn't make excuses."

Randy said he noticed other things about Larry that separated him from the pack of other drivers.

"He was the most prepared guy I've ever seen," Randy said. "If you had a big show, Larry was one of the first cars there. I don't think he ever fully understood why some people unloaded their car, jacked it up and started working on them in the pits." Randy said when Larry arrived, his car was ready to hit the racetrack.

"There was another thing about Larry: He could drive on asphalt and he could drive on dirt," Randy said. "If we had a one-mile drag strip with gravel I have no doubt he would have successfully driven on that too."

Randy credits Larry with filling the seats, even today, because of everything he did.

"I believe the reason the Late Models are so strong here and have survived is because of Larry," he said. "I honestly believe they are still strong today because of him."

A DIFFERENT SIDE OF LARRY

Charley Hurley, who worked for Dayco LLC, an automotive belt manufacturer, was good friends with Larry. Charley balanced engines for Larry and was the also the tech man at the Fairgrounds Speedway in Springfield for many years.

Dayco wanted to test its belts and Charley suggested testing them in a race car. He also suggested that Dayco sponsor Larry's car. Before long, Dayco became Larry's second sponsor. Charley said Larry ran Dayco's test belts and had trouble at first. But Dayco kept improving them and the engineers would tension them for him. "Soon, he could run a one-hundred lap race with no belt trouble," Charley said.

In 1967, Larry received one thousand dollars to test Dayco's belts. He also received uniforms for all the drivers and four brand new Good year Race Tires. Larry helped them developed a belt that would not turn over in hard acceleration.

"Larry was a hard guy to get to know but if he liked you, he was your friend for life," Charley said. "Not too many people know this, but my wife Helen came down with cancer in the early 2001. They found out she had spinal cancer and was going be in a wheelchair for the rest of her life.

"When Larry found out she had cancer he called me and asked if he could come see Helen at her bedside. She always liked Larry but was kind of afraid of him because of his rough demeanor," Charley said." He sat on one side of the bed and Judy sat on the other side. They held her hands and Larry said, 'I want you to know that you can beat this. If someone like me can beat it, you can beat it too.' That meant more to Helen than anything else. Helen loved Larry to death after that day."

Charley, a member of Larry's pit crew, said Larry was compassionate and loved kids. One night, when he went to Rolla with the crew, Larry won the trophy dash and received a small trophy. He also won the feature that night and received a large trophy.

"A man brought his little boy down to the pits after the race," Charley said. "He said, 'Larry I want you to meet my son' and Larry shook the boy's hand. Larry asked him if he liked the racing and the boy said 'Yes, you are my favorite driver.'" Larry told Charley go get the trophy he had just won. 'I asked, 'Which one?' And Larry said 'the big one of course.' Larry handed it to the kid. Larry gave his trophies to the kids many times."

UNBEATABLE RECORD

James Ince said he doubts anyone will ever beat Larry's record of five national championships.

"I don't think that part of it is possible," he said. "I'm not sure that people necessarily appreciate how hard that was to do. For years, when we were doing it, a lot in this area heard that there was no competition and it was a set-up deal. But the reality of life, like in 1992, we won thirty-eight out of forty races. I challenge anybody just to keep a car together in that many races and keep something from breaking that many times. He got a lot of respect in the latter part of his career that he didn't get in the early part. And that's great but I don't think people really appreciate how much effort, time and work went into that and the challenge that it was. But, no, I … can't see

Dan Mahoney collection

Larry Phillips headed for another feature win at I-44 Speedway in Lebanon, Missouri.

where that would ever be surpassed."

YOU CAN'T FIX STUPID

"You can go to college and you can get a degree; you can do a lot of things in life, but you can't fix stupid," James said. "Larry was a very, very smart guy, and he always figured it out. He wasn't ever in a position to say, 'Okay, that worked,' but he wanted to know why it worked. He wanted to make it better the next time and again. I don't think people fully understand that's how he paid the bills. It had to get better; it wasn't going to be second best. It was very, very hard, and it is to this day, to make a living in racing, especially if you're not doing NASCAR on a higher level."

"Larry would just figure it out. He is one of the smartest people I've ever known. Maybe near genius on some levels," James said. "I mean the reality of life is he did just about everything he ever decided to do. The day he decided he wanted to fly helicopters, he learned to fly helicopters and not only that, he built one himself. So he was an extremely sharp individual to the point that he was compulsive about things. Once he got his mind set on something, there could be a week that he would go without sleeping until he got that project figured out or completed. I don't think many people ever saw that side of him. And for the guys around him, when I was working for him, I mean, he all but killed me … There was no doubt about it, he'd work you to death."

THE BEST AND THE WORST
"It's very hard being around anybody in life who is a perfectionist," James said. "I mean, that part of it is really hard to do. But I sure got a whole lot more in return than I had to give out. For Terry Gene, he was in the family and its just the way he knew it, so there was no doubt that he was very hard to get along with. I described him for years as the best and the worst. He was the hardest person you could ever be around. But at the same time if you ever got through and got to know him, he was the best person you could ever be around. He had the biggest heart of anybody I ever knew."

James said he eventually had to choose between working for Larry and moving on so that he could make a living in racing.

"Well … it all goes back to me actually getting married," he said. "The plan and the direction was that I was actually going to go drive Ford cars for Larry; there was a future there. It was kind of funny and one of those life moments that we were actually building my car when I got married, and when I got back from my honeymoon, he had sold it, and that was the end of the conversation.

"So we got to the end of the year and my wife actually informed me that, if I was going to race, I needed to make money doing it. I needed to come to North Carolina, and I made a deal with her: We'd come down [to North Carolina], talk to people, and we'd see how it worked out. And if I went to work and I didn't like it, I'd give it five years and I could go back to what I wanted to do because I always believed I needed to be driving race cars. You know, I realized I couldn't afford to do it on the level on my own. So when we left after the championship in 1992 on Saturday night, I went and talked to Larry that Sunday which was one of the hardest things I've ever done. And Monday morning we drove to North Carolina, and by Wednesday I had a job for Bobby Labonte for his Busch Team. The following Monday, I started working for him, and things just kind of progressed from there. I was really fortunate in my career for the things that let me advance as fast as I did through the sport. I believe it was the work ethic and the things that Larry bestowed on me, especially the work ethic and coming from Springfield. I just honestly outworked everybody down here and I really put that much effort into it."

Judy Phillips collection

Larry and Judy Phillips attend a private dinner on October 1, 1996, the night before the 1996 NASCAR Winston Racing Series Championship awards ceremony in Nashville, Tennessee.

NASCAR collection

Sportsman Pickup Covers was Larry Phillips' main sponsor through the years. Here, Larry shows off one of their caps.

Larry Phillips, No. 75, takes the lead from Jamie McMurray, No. 15, at I-44 Speedway in Lebanon, Missouri.

Larry Phillips takes another feature win at I-44 Speedway in Lebanon, Missouri.

Dan Mahoney collection

Larry Phillips, center, inspects the front end of his car after it was damaged during a race.

Photo by Kendall Bell

The monument of the Ozarks Area Racers Association at the Fairgrounds, site of the former Fairgrounds Speedway, in Springfield, Missouri, bears the names of all drivers who were inducted as either Legends or Pioneers.

Larry Phillips waits to check in to the pits at I-44 Speedway in Lebanon, Missouri.

Dan Mahoney collection

Dan Mahoney collection

Larry Phillips in his "office."

Dan Mahoney collection

Larry Phillips, left, at Ascot Park in Los Angeles, California, in 1979, after a race.

Another promotional photo of Larry Phillips on the backstretch at the Fairgrounds Speedway in Springfield, Missouri.

Larry Phillips racing at the Fairgrounds Speedway in Springfield, Missouri, in 1975.

Bob & LLoretta Williams collection

Judy and Larry Phillips at the Ozarks Area Racers Association banquet.

Dan Mahoney collection

Larry Phillips, racing at Bolivar Speedway USA, honors Wayne McCarthy, who was killed during a race, by displaying McCarthy's No. 28 on the rear window.

Larry Phillips hot lapping at I-44 Speedway in Lebanon, Missouri.

Larry Phillips races at Ascot Park in Los Angeles in 1979.

Photos from the Dan Mahoney collection

Dan Mahoney collection

Larry Phillips, driving No. 75, leads Steve Simmons, No. 19, and others at Speedway USA in Bolivar, Missouri, in 1995.

Dan Mahoney collection

Larry Phillips at the Bolivar Speedway USA in Bolivar, Missouri, on True Value night.

Larry Phillips in his asphalt car—a Camaro.

Larry Phillips smiles after another feature win

Judy Phillips collection

Larry Phillips poses with two of his greatest loves: his helicopter and his race car.

Dan Mahoney collection

Larry Phillips slides into Turn One on his roof over No. 21 Ken Dickinson's race car during a 1993 race at I-44 Speedway.

Larry Phillips, No 75, Doug Aasby, No. 2, and Dale Roper, No. 28, go three-wide during a 1999 race At Bolivar Speedway USA in Bolivar, Missouri.

Larry Phillips takes a smoke as he sits on the track during a red flag.

Photos from the Dan Mahoney collection

It was a common sight to see Larry Phillips pose with a trophy queen following yet another win.

Photos from the Dan Mahoney collection

Larry Phillips, No. 75, and Jamie McMurray, No 25, at Bolivar Speedway USA in Bolivar, Missouri, in 1999.

Larry Phillips "dirt tracking" at Ascot Park in Los Angeles, California, in 1979.

Larry Phillips' Independent Stave-sponsored Late Model dirt car.

Larry Phillips, left, and Ernie Irvan, who later became a NASCAR Winston Cup driver, battle it out on the track in Stockton, California.

Larry Phillips wins a Modified Main event at Bolivar Speedway USA at Bolivar, Missouri, in 1999.

Judy Phillips collection

Here's a picture of Larry Phillips' promotional Sportsman Pickup Covers photograph.

Dan Mahoney collection

Larry Phillips drove Marc Reno's No. 1 Camaro in California several times in 1982.

Larry Phillips poses with a trophy queen following another victory in 1998.

Photos from the Dan Mahoney collection

Larry Phillips runs a race in 1995.

And the winner is ... Larry Phillips!

Larry Phillips races for first place at Ascot Park in Los Angeles, California, with track champion Jim Neal.

Larry Phillips poses at his new shop in Springfield, Missouri.

Larry Phillips often used hot laps to determine his car's setup for the race.

Larry Phillips speeds past the crowd during a race.

Larry Phillips smiles for camera with his No. 75 Sportsman Pickup Cover Pontiac.

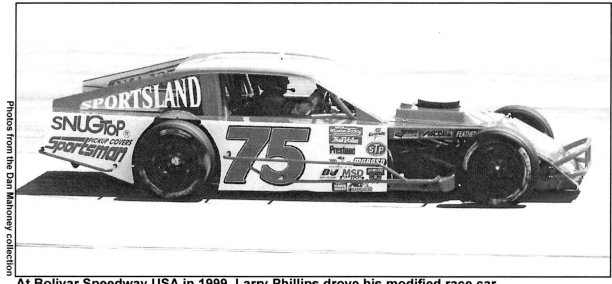

Photos from the Dan Mahoney collection

At Bolivar Speedway USA in 1999, Larry Phillips drove his modified race car.

Terry Phillips, Larry Phillips' son, takes a hard turn into the corner in the Don Babb, Andy's Frozen Custard dirt car.

Larry Phillips carries the US flag on the parade lap at the Fourth of July Special race.

Photos from the Dan Mahoney collection

Charles Hurley collection

Don Kordalis and Larry Phillips pose as they discuss racing strategy.

Dan Mahoney collection

Larry Phillips, in front, Ernie Irvan and Rusty Wallace fight for the lead during a race.

Larry Phillips after a win in O'Reilly Auto Parts Winners Circle in 1999.

Larry Phillips, No. 75, and Chuck Becker Jr., driving No. 29, racing at Mesa Martin Raceway in Bakersfield, California.

Photos from the Dan Mahoney collection

Putting the race car back upright did almost as much damage as the original flip did. Larry Phillips flipped it during a race at I-44 Speedway in Lebanon, Missouri.

Photos from the Dan Mahoney collection

Larry Phillips, No. 75, leads Rusty Wallace, in the No. 55 car, during a race.

CHAPTER SIXTEEN
End of an Era

Larry competed three more full seasons, and remained a factor in the point races. He placed sixth in the regional points race in 1997; third in 1998; and sixth in 1999, and added a total of thirty-one more feature wins.

CANCER STRIKES

Larry was diagnosed with lung cancer in 2000 but continued to race. He posted three wins, the third coming on June 3, which would become the final feature win of his career. He posted a seventh-place finish the following week, but a disagreement with track officials over a restart position in that race aggravated him more than he wanted to be aggravated by racing at the time. With his energy being sapped by chemotherapy, he decided to simply stop.

Larry returned to Lebanon one more time the following year. He raced in the 2001 season-opening event at the track on April 7. He led the feature until late in the race, when he tired and was passed by Ken Dickinson, who took the win. Larry finished second.

Larry left the speedway that night knowing that he would not return, and that he could not return. His health would no longer allow him to show up at the track, confident he was signing in at the pit gate with everything he needed to win. Without that confidence, he would not go racing again.

"In the beginning, it was pretty bad," Judy said. "He had his first treatment, which was a week long. He had to go there every day for a week. He went to Texas for a second opinion. I think that really bothered him when they told him that what they were doing in Springfield is what they would do down there … That really bothered him because he thought that going to Texas would be a miracle, you know, because of that being a cancer. He quit smoking when he couldn't breathe anymore. I think he wished he'd never started, but he said he enjoyed smoking, and he said he was going to smoke until he couldn't.

"After his treatments and everything, for like a year and a half, he kind of started getting better. He had a pretty positive attitude. I was around him so much there at the last, you know, like the last year … I knew he was getting worse, and he knew he was getting worse. When they finally told him that they had done all that they could do, he still didn't give up … Every day he planned something, I mean, he talked about the future and stuff."

Tommy Joe Pauschert said his friendship with Larry didn't end with the drop of a checkered flag.

"After Larry had quit racing and I had stopped racing, he called me one night and said he heard I was going to a lot of motorcycle shows and asked if he could tag along.

"I said I'd be happy for him to go. One of my friends from Missouri had been a flagman, and he and Larry never got along. Bill Crooks had gone to the tracks ever since I had been racing. I called him and told him Larry Phillips called and wanted to go to Daytona with us. He said, 'Really?' He said, 'Aw man, I believe I'll stay at home.'"

"I said, 'No, you're not going to stay at home. We're going to go, and all of us are going to have fun.' We went and laughed and had a fun time and after that, everywhere we went to a motorcycle show, Larry went with us. We just really had a fun time. I never traveled with anybody any more pleasant to travel with from then on. We had a lot of fun and became really good friends."

Although the wives sometimes went along, it was usually just the guys, he said.

"We all had motor homes at the time, and we'd pull the motorcycles on a trailer because that way we'd have a place to stay when we got there.

"We all traveled together. Anytime we were going south or east, Larry would come to my shop and we'd leave from there. He'd visit with my mom and dad a little bit and then we'd take off and do our own thing."

At night the conversation always turned back to their racing memories.

"Yeah, we raced every night," Tommy Joe said with a laugh. "We talked about the races, and Larry knew a lot of people. I always enjoyed his stories about the different people. Sometimes they'd be people I knew; other times not. But Larry could really tell a story.

"I loved the story he always told about Smokey Unich. He was a legendary motor builder. Larry got a motor from him and, to hear Larry tell it, it was the worst motor he'd ever had in his life. He'd tell us about it and laugh."

There was one thing Tommy Joe said took him a long time to understand about Larry: "He'd buy a car and the first thing he'd do is cut it up. He'd redo it, redo the front end and then go racing. And I don't know of a car he ever had that he didn't change. I don't care who built the car. I can remember that from the NDRA and even on asphalt. He'd tell us about the different asphalt cars he had. He'd cut the front end of them off. He'd get a race car from somebody and, before he'd get to the race track he'd decide to cut the front end off of it and change it."

Tommy Joe admired Larry's racing style.

"He was very gifted in the field of racing," he said. "I don't know that anybody else drove exactly like Larry. He was definitely a runner up front. If anybody every drove as hard as Larry it would have probably been Larry Moore (a driver who was inducted into the National Dirt Driver Hall of Fame). Larry Moore drove awful hard in a race car. He was a hard racer. And that was good. I mean he just drove hard."

"Larry was as good of a car builder as he was a driver, maybe even more so. Larry was so,

Larry Phillips takes a smoke as he sits on the track during a red flag.

Dan Mahoney collection

so smart on car parts and what they did," Joe said. "He helped so many people get started."

Tommy Joe said, later on, he and Larry began traveling together to various motorcycle shows.

He said each man respected the other, although they remained fierce competitors on the track

Over the next few years, Larry enjoyed motorcycle riding and attended Bike Week events in Daytona Beach with his wife and friends.

After Larry quit racing, he sometimes watched his friends race on television.

"He watched a lot after Rusty and Mark and Ken Schrader got into it," Judy said. "He watched it a little bit before that but not a lot."

Some people might be surprised to learn that Larry once raced motorcycles.

"In the seventies he did a lot of motorcycle riding," Judy said. "I would go with him then, and we would go to Chadwick (a town in Missouri). When we went down there the first time, it had rained that weekend and the little creek, the little rivers and streams and stuff, we had to cross them. Larry crossed one just fine, and he said, 'Let's find a more shallow place for you to come across,' because he was afraid my motorcycle would drown out because his almost did.

"So we go on down, and he's on one side of the creek and I'm on the other side, and we're

Dan Mahoney collection

Larry Phillips determines his race strategy.

just talking. It's not very wide.

"We finally found a place for me to cross," she said. "I think my motorcycle sunk. It didn't even have the ground under it. But he thought it was shallow there. We had to turn it upside down. It took us forever to get it restarted because by then, we were quite a ways from the truck, too far to push. I was sopping wet. It was cold out, but you've got to be tough if you're going to do it. You either do it or you don't do it. Do it, do it right, or stay home."

MOTORCYCLE WRECK

One evening, tragedy struck as Judy and Larry were riding motorcycles. Judy took a curve wide and sideswiped an oncoming vehicle. Judy's leg had to be amputated. She still remembers every detail of that dreadful night.

"We were going to go down to Pomme de Terre [Lake] on a Friday night," she said. "I came home from work that day and took a nap because I was really tired, and then he came in and asked me if I wanted a bite to eat, and I said, 'Yeah.' We were going to a restaurant on the lake to have the best catfish."

Judy was driving a Honda, and Larry had a Harley-Davidson.

"There was a lot of traffic that day, it was just unreal," she said. "Of course, Larry was going down there at a pretty good pace, you know, and I was trying to keep up, and he passed this eighteen-wheeler. I wouldn't pass where he passed, so I waited for a stretch of highway where it was straight.

"I finally got it and I speeded up and went around him, but when I went around I missed the sign that says it was a hairpin curve up ahead. Of course I could see that there was a corner, but I didn't realize that it was a stop-and-go corner.

"I got to that corner and I was going too fast and I just ran into the side of a Mustang. I was watching Larry and I could see him watching me. I was more concerned about him not watching where he was going because of all the traffic." Judy said the collision didn't knock her from the bike.

"I just hit the car and then tried to ride it over to the edge of the ditch, but I couldn't stop the bike because I couldn't take it out of gear," she said. "And I had hurt my hand. He was watching me through his rear view mirror and he saw it happen."

She knew Larry wouldn't buy her another bike if she messed that one up. She was more concerned about the motorcycle and Larry's reaction, than she was about her own injuries.

"I didn't know that I was hurt that bad until they told me at the hospital that they would have to amputate my leg below my knee. I was devastated. I was in the hospital for seven or eight weeks.

"There was a lady that came to see me in the hospital. Her name was Janell Coppage, and she was from Bolivar, but she lives in Kansas City now … and she had lost her leg when she was eleven. She had on a skirt and a pair of sandals, and she was just all friendly and happy but came

Dennis Slane collection

Larry Phillips cruises around the track.

over and sat down by me and she said, 'You didn't even see my leg did you?' And I said, 'No I didn't see it.' And she lifted her leg up and it looked really nice. She was wearing a prosthetic. [She was a] super nice person, and she gave me a whole new outlook on my future. I really appreciated her. I thank her to this day."

Dale Roper, a former competitor, said Larry felt awful about the accident.

"He blamed himself for that," Roper said. "He had bought the motorcycle for her. He said, halfway into the turn, he realized she was going faster than she needed to go."

"Larry took very good care of me after I came home, even though the chemo and radiation was taking its toll on him," Judy said.

Dan Mahoney collection

Larry Phillips talks horsepower with engine builder Jim Ruble.

Dan Mahoney collection

Larry Phillips smiles after receiving his awards at the NASCAR Winston Racing Series Banquet in 1995.

CHAPTER SEVENTEEN
Simply the Best

Friends say that back in 2000 when Larry was diagnosed with lung cancer, his remaining lifespan could be measured in only weeks. Over the next four years, he enjoyed life the way he wanted to enjoy it, good and bad.

Tommy Joe Pauschert said he'll always remember the shock of learning that Larry had cancer.

"Bill Crooks from Springfield called me and told me," Tommy Joe said. "I think Larry had told it at a race track. He told the crowd he was sick and was going to be gone for awhile."

Tommy Joe said Larry changed dramatically after he learned about the cancer.

"For three and a half years he wasn't Larry Phillips, the racer. He was Larry Phillips, someone else. He was a lot of fun to be with. But you know, I think I liked him better the other way when he raced.

"Another good friend of mine, Michael Standridge, was a psychologist. He went with us on all of the motorcycle trips. And he and Larry talked a lot. Larry would talk about the cancer, and I remember him saying how much he regretted taking the treatments. He said if he had known back then what he knew now he'd just take what time he had left and live it out instead of going through the suffering and all of that."

Tommy Joe said Larry usually got what he wanted. But there was one thing that eluded him: "Larry always wanted to go with us to Sturgis, South Dakota.

"It seemed like he never could get there," Tommy Joe said. "I went every year. But something always came up for Larry. Most of the time he was sick from his chemo treatment and he just couldn't go.

"I'll always remember I got a call that Larry had gotten pretty bad. I decided I'd go see him. I got up at three that morning and drove to Springfield to see him in the hospital."

Tommy Joe said Judy and a lot of Larry's other family members were there when he arrived.

"He was really glad to see me," Tommy Joe said. "He told me how sorry he was that he wasn't going to be able to go up to Sturgis with us. I said, 'Aw Larry, don't worry about it. We'll go next year.'

"He really wanted to go and said he appreciated me asking him and he appreciated me

Motorcycles lead Larry Phillips' funeral procession on September 21, 2004, through Springfield. It was almost as if the entire community turned out to mourn their fallen hero.

being his friend."

Two days later, on September 21, 2004, Larry died.

More than a thousand people attended Larry's funeral. A hundred motorcycle friends were more noticeable than all the racing people there. Most of those bikers led the procession from the church to the cemetery.

Dale Roper was one of the people who spoke at Larry's funeral.

"One of the best stories about Larry I told at his funeral," he said. "ARTGO was having a mid-week race in Cedar Rapids, Iowa. (Editor's note: A man named Art Frigo created the series with the help of two friends. He came up with the name by taking his first full name and the last two letters of his last name: ARTGO.) John Carnes, promoter for ARTGO called to ask Larry to run there. He had all volunteer help. He called Ike 'Richard' Icenhower and asked if he would go with him. Larry picked him up and headed up the road. The first time they stopped to eat, they realized they had left their glasses behind. ... Larry was going to check the tire pressure, he said, 'Richard, check the tire pressure. You hold the gauge and I will stand over your shoulder and read it.' A guy standing nearby said, 'You're going to be out there racing and can't see?' Larry said, 'Don't worry, sonny, I can see to the end of the hood.' He lacked one car of lapping the entire field that night."

SIMPLY THE BEST
James Ince said his relationship with Larry was special to both of them.

"I feel like we were very close and I just can't describe him. There's too many things we went through or talked about or did that for me to be able to sum him up in a few words is almost impossible other than saying, 'he was simply the best' and it's as simple as that."

Wreaths depicting Larry Phillips' now-famous No. 75 filled the flower trucks on the day of his funeral.

Dennis Slane collection

Longtime Larry Phillips fans might remember that he enjoyed racing dirt bikes at the Fairgrounds in Springfield, Missouri, in the '60s.

CHAPTER EIGHTEEN
The Media Remember Larry

Lyndal Scranton, sports editor for the *Springfield News-Leader*; Bill Breshears, sports editor for the *Bolivar Herald-Free Press*; and Ned Reynolds, sports director and anchor for KY3 TV, an NBC affiliate in Springfield, recalled their memories of Larry Phillips.

Lyndal wrote many stories about Larry during Larry's storied career. He was a fan for many years before becoming a journalist.

"Larry's shop was about a block-and-a-half from the house I grew up in," Lyndal said. "I was probably seven or eight years old and I remember race car motors going all hours of the day and night.

"We started going to races at Fairgrounds [Speedway] to see the guy who was winning most of the races out there. I finally put two and two together and realized it was the guy whose shop was near our house.

"I became a fan just from seeing him up close and seeing the car up close."

Larry had a reputation for staying focused on his cars and often told people to leave if he was busy. But Lyndal said he never experienced that.

"I remember he told us one day we were all being quiet and he really appreciated that. He said he really enjoyed having us around."

"One day he gave us a bunch of stickers and decals—STP stickers and whatever he had lying around. I was really proud of them."

Lyndal said already knowing Larry helped when he began covering races for the newspaper.

"That made it a lot more meaningful. I kept up with his races when I was a teenager at the Fairgrounds [Speedway]. We traveled to Rolla or I-70 Speedway to see him race.

"I had been at the paper maybe five or six years and the guy who covered racing took another job so I moved right into the racing beat. I was the only one on the staff who had an interest in racing.

"I covered Larry's last race at Fairgrounds [Speedway] about 1986 or '87. I remember Davey Allison was there for the ARCA race."

Even though Lyndal was a fan, he strived to maintain impartiality in his stories regarding Larry. And on at least one occasion, Larry took exception with a story.

"He got into a ruckus up at Lebanon [Speedway] one year, and I wrote some stuff about that and he called me on the phone all upset about how I misconstrued him. I said, 'Larry, I'm just going on the facts the people who were there gave me in direct quotes. I tried to report both sides of it.'"

Larry accepted Lyndal's word and moved on without bringing it up again.

Lyndal said, just as Larry had little time for gossip at his shop, he had even less time for reporters who walked in without an appointment.

"You couldn't just show up at his shop unannounced and think you were going to get an interview. I called him one day wanting to talk and he told me to come to his shop about one o'clock the following day."

Lyndal arrived and found Larry working beneath a race car.

"How long is this going to take?" Larry asked.

"I told him about ten minutes," Lyndal said. "He told me to give him about five minutes and he'd be finished. A few minutes later, Terry asked me if Larry knew I was coming. I told him I had made an appointment a day earlier. He went over and talked with Larry. Just a few minutes after that, Larry came out and we talked for about an hour. He had forgotten I was coming. He was as nice as anyone could be.

> *"One thing about Larry, if he knew you knew what you were talking about, that you had done your homework, he'd respect that and would talk with you. Before a race, you never went up to Larry, though. You just didn't bother him before a race."*
> **—Lyndal Scranton, *Springfield News-Leader* Sports Reporter**

"One thing about Larry, if he knew you knew what you were talking about, that you had done your homework, he'd respect that and would talk with you. Before a race, you never went up to Larry, though. You just didn't bother him before a race.

"Larry had what I call a 'blue-collar' work ethic. He demanded excellence of himself and didn't expect to run second in any race he ran."

Lyndal said the Larry Phillips he knew was always gracious, but he became even more so after learning he had terminal cancer.

"I don't know if you'd say a softer side came out, but that's how it seemed."

Lyndal said Larry's death had a profound effect on both the local racing scene and the area.

"The community reaction went beyond sports," he said.

The newspaper set up a special place on its website for people to send condolences and comment.

"We had more hits on that site than anything we've done before or since then," Lyndal said.

Just as many of Dale Earnhardt's fans began pulling for Dale Jr. after the elder Earnhardt was killed, many of Larry's fans embraced his son, Terry, Lyndal said.

Larry would be proud of the racer Terry has become, he said.

"Terry's better at marketing and meeting his fans," Lyndal said. "Larry never cared at all about selling T-shirts. All he cared about was winning a race."

BILL BRESHEARS
Bill Breshears, sports editor of the *Bolivar Herald-Free Press* in Bolivar, Missouri, followed Larry's racing career for many years.

"In the late 1960s, I believe it was, as a teenager I attended one of my first races at the Fairgrounds Speedway in Springfield. After the regular racing program, they had a 'Powder Puff Race' where wives, girlfriends, friends, etcetera, drove the cars.

"Larry Phillips' red number 75 1962 Chevrolet was one of the cars entered. The driver started at the back of the pack, passed a couple of cars, then spun out over the east end of the track.

"Turns One and Two were built up and open, so there was quite a hill to descend once your car left the track. And it was the same on Turns Three and Four. The driver drove back over the hump that was Turn Two and caught back up with the field.

"After catching the field, the driver started fish-tailing, spinning and again went off the track, this time on the west end. The car came roaring back onto the track, caught the field, passed its way into first place and spun out again. This time it went off the east end.

"On the final lap, number 75 caught back up with the pack, fish-tailed and finished dead last in the Powder Puff.

"The crowd was entertained and anxious to see who was 'driving' Larry's car. The driver got out, removed a long brown wig and waved to the crowd. You guessed it: It was none other than Larry Phillips himself!

"This was early in Larry's racing career. He went on to win five Winston Racing Series Championships. He had his detractors over the years, as do all winners; but on this 1960s evening in Springfield, he won over a lot of fans for a lifetime, including me."

NED REYNOLDS
Ned Reynolds has been with KY3-TV in Springfield since 1967, and is one of the foremost sports anchors in the region.

In 1974, he was the announcer at the Fairgrounds Speedway in Springfield.

"When Larry Phillips was on the track, he made darned sure that he was in first place, not second," Ned said.

He said Larry was among the hardest-nosed competitors in any sport he has ever covered. "He was a one of a kind," Ned said.

He recalled a time at the Fairgrounds Speedway when promoters brought in Bobby Allison, but Larry beat him soundly.

"He also mentored other drivers such as Mark Martin and Rusty Wallace," Ned said.

Even though the races with Martin and Wallace were competitive, Larry won most of the time, he said.

Although Larry was a tough competitor, Larry was gentlemanly and nice anytime he was interviewed.

Ned presented Larry's induction into the Missouri Sports Hall of Fame.

Larry Phillips'

NASCAR Winston Racing Series

Records by Year

Larry Phillips' NASCAR Winston Racing Series Career Records

Year	Starts	Wins	Top 5s	Top 10s	Point Fund Awards	Tracks
1989*	27	23	25	27	$62,000	Lebanon/Bolivar#
1990	6	3	—	—	$0	Lebanon/Bolivar
1991*	40	32	35	37	$70,250	Lakeside#/1-70/Lebanon
1992*	40	38	38	39	$77.750	Lakeside#/I-70/Leb./Bolivar
1993**	30	23	25	26	$25,250	Leb.#/Bol./I-70/Lakeside
1994**	35	27	30	32	$31,750	Lebanon#/Bolivar#
1995*	40	32	38	39	$100,650	Lebanon#/Bolivar#
1996*	20	14	18	18	$114,000	Lebanon#/Bolivar#
1997	16	7	15	16	$ 5,100	Lebanon/Bolivar#
1998	19	12	16	17	$ 11,850	Lebanon#/Bolivar#
1999	17	12	17	17	$ 5,100	Lebanon/Bolivar#
2000	7	3	5	6	$0	Lebanon
2001	1	0	1	1	$0	Lebanon
Totals:	308	226	263	275	$503,700	

Key: * = national championship; **= regional championship; # = track championship.
5 national championships; 7 regional championships; 13 track championships.
13-year NASCAR career winning percentage: .734.
13-year NASCAR career finishes outside the top 10: 33 in 308 starts.

Larry Phillips' NASCAR Winston Racing Series Records by Year

1989 Regional Point Standings

Mid-America Region

Driver	Points	Starts	Wins	Top 5s	Top 10s
1. Larry Phillips	**3600**	**27**	**23**	**25**	**27**
2. Mike Love	3600	44	20	40	44
3. Steve Murgic	3495	43	11	26	36
4. Chuck Winders	3465	27	11	24	24
5. Kirk Shaw	3440	37	7	29	32
6. Dwain Behrens	3420	43	7	28	29
7. Frank Reaber	3390	37	8	23	35
8. Frank Kimmel	3380	33	3	24	29
9. Jason Keller	3370	32	5	22	28
10 Steve Coker	3340	41	4	23	35

Central Region

Driver	Points	Starts	Wins	Top 5s	Top 10s
1. Ray Guss Jr.	3600	53	38	48	51
2. Joe Kosiski	3600	37	21	35	36
3. Steve Kosiski	3530	44	13	40	42
4. Steve Fraise	3490	54	10	27	32
5. Curt Martin	3490	54	9	41	45
6. Terry Gallaher	3475	43	8	34	40
7. Ed Kosiski	3465	51	7	38	43
8. Dave Chase	3380	45	6	20	31
9. Mark Burgtorf	3365	39	6	20	31
10. Rollie Frink	3335	50	2	33	42

Eastern Seaboard Region

Driver	Points	Starts	Wins	Top 5s	Top 10s
1. Jimmy Hatchell	3545	21	15	21	21
2. David Into	3540	22	16	22	22
3. Sean Graham	3475	21	17	17	19
4. Jack Sprague	3463	22	15	19	19
5. Michael Rowe	3336	21	10	17	18
6. Eddie Goodson III	3334	21	9	15	29
7. Robert Elliott	3316	21	3	17	21
8. David Bilbrey	3291	21	5	17	21
9. Phil Elvis	3284	22	3	16	21
10. Leland Prewitt	3265	21	3	17	20

Great Northern Region

Driver	Points	Starts	Wins	Top 5s	Top 10s
1. Kevin Nuttleman	3525	21	14	21	21
2. Arnie Wheatcroft	3510	22	22	22	22
3. Steve Peles	3460	21	10	20	21
4. Cart Zaretzke	3445	22	6	21	22
5. Nick Carlson	3435	22	7	19	20
6. Lloyd Sims	3430	22	5	22	22
7. Kelly Tanner	3428	22	10	19	21
8. Marv Bohling Jr.	3411	21	9	18	21
9. Ray Wallace	3358	22	7	19	21
10.John Vallo	3364	22	9	17	21

Sunbelt Region

Driver	Points	Starts	Wins	Top 5s	Top 10s
1. Paul White	3465	22	10	20	22
2. Terry Lackey	3396	22	9	18	21
3. Tobin Whitt	3371	22	5	19	20
4. Ed Hale	3342	22	7	19	20
5. Erik Gibson	3338	22	12	15	18
6. David Browning Jr.	3307	21	9	16	18
7. Jerry Goodwin	3307	22	4	17	22
8. David Rogers	3301	22	8	16	17
9. Tony Walls	3293	21	4	18	19
10. David Dulock	3252	21	4	16	19

Pacific Coast Region

Driver	Points	Starts	Wins	Top 5s	Top 10s
1. Bobby Hogge	3550	20	15	20	20
2. Jeff Silva	3540	20	14	20	20
3. Jim Pettit II	3540	20	14	20	20
4. Steve Hendren	3385	20	5	20	20
5. Ed Sans Jr.	3380	20	4	20	20
6. Rock Belden	3362	20	5	19	20
7. Tim Gillit	3340	20	4	20	20
8. Ron Ratteree	3310	20	7	16	20
9. Ed Gibber	3300	20	2	20	20
10. Ken Boyd	3292	20	7	17	18

Mid-Atlantic Region

Driver	Points	Starts	Wins	Top 5s	Top 10s
1. Bob Pressley	3520	43	13	29	36
2. Roy Hendrick	3485	39	12	23	33
3. Robert Huffman	3470	41	9	31	35
4. Charlie Ford, Jr.	3435	36	5	26	29
5. Larry Ogle	3430	38	5	34	35
6. Randy Porter	3385	25	8	18	22
7. Phil Warren	3375	43	4	29	39
8. Bugs Hairfield	3335	34	3	19	25
9. Eddie Johnson	3310	39	5	20	24
10. Maurice Hill	3294	23	7	16	17

Northeast Region

Driver	Points	Starts	Wins	Top 5s	Top 10s
1. Jan Leaty	3415	30	8	22	24
2. Reggie Ruggiero	3410	26	7	20	23
3. Michael Murphy	329	20	5	17	19
4. Jerry Marquis	3306	30	8	16	20
5. Bruce D'Allessandro	3290	28	2	19	24
6. Mike Christopher	3254	20	6	17	18
7. John Branscombe	3222	20	4	15	19
8. Dan Avery	3125	21	4	13	17
9. Wayne Helliwell	3081	21	3	12	16	-0-

1991 Regional Point Standings

Mid-America Region

Driver	Points	Starts	Wins	Top 5s	Top 10s
1. Larry Phillips	**3600**	**40**	**32**	**35**	**37**
2. Mike Love	3570	35	17	31	34
3. Steve Murgic	3540	42	14	26	35
4. John Vallo	3535	40	14	28	38
5. Russell Phillips	3445	39	8	23	29
6. Robbie Dean	3420	29	7	21	26
7. Chuck Winders	3410	39	3	26	34
8. Dick Dunlevy Jr.	3400	39	3	26	34
10. Gene Claxton	3395	31	3	23	30

Mid-Atlantic Region

Driver	Points	Starts	Wins	Top 5s	Top 10s
1. Johnny Rumley	3600	41	20	31	34
2. Eddie Johnson	3570	41	17	33	34
3. Barry Beggerly	3510	43	11	33	38
4. Max Prestwood Jr.	3457	22	12	18	19
5. Roy Hendrick	3455	33	8	23	28
6. Maurice Hill	3450	29	11	22	26
7. Jay Fogleman	3450	49	8	27	42
8. Larry Ogle	3450	35	7	28	33
9. Jeff Agnew	3450	44	5	35	37
10. Todd Massey	3440	48	7	32	41

Sunbelt Region

Driver	Points	Starts	Wins	Top 5s	Top 10s
1. David Rogers	3570	22	17	22	22
2. Howard Willis III	3494	21	15	19	20
3. Dick Cobb	3458	22	13	19	20
4. John Borneman Jr.	3402	22	13	17	19
5. Chuck Miinch	3400	22	7	20	20
6. Bruce Shaw	3391	22	8	19	21
7. Jason Oates	3372	22	4	19	22
8. Tuck Trentham	3360	22	3	19	22
9. Tony Walls	3356	22	6	17	22
10. George Hagy	3346	22	7	18	21

Great Northern Region

Driver	Points	Starts	Wins	Top 5s	Top 10s
1. Eddy McKean	3520	22	14	22	22
2. Kevin Nuttleman	3480	22	12	20	21
3. Roger Gannon	3411	22	12	17	22
4. Mark Hubbard	3375	21	5	20	21
5. Bobby Wilberg	3331	22	3	19	21
6. Craig Raudman	3321	22	3	18	21
7. Jeff Hikemeyer	3320	21	5	17	19
8. Gary Lewis	3318	22	8	16	18
9. Ricky Bilderback	3283	22	6	16	18
10. Dennis Miller	3260	22	7	18	21

Northeast Region

Driver	Points	Starts	Wins	Top 5s	Top 10s
1. Jerry Marquis	3520	38	13	31	37
2. Glenn Gault	3510	42	11	35	39
3. Bob Sibila	3405	41	7	22	31
4. Tim Ice	3340	34	3	20	26
5. Buck Catalano	3306	34	5	16	23
6. Charlie Cragan	3237	42	4	15	32
7. Steve Peles	3235	22	5	17	19
8. Dan Mason	3199	29	3	13	23
9. Rick Miller	3140	39	2	13	24
10. Norm Wrenn	3140	21	1	13	18

Central Region

Driver	Points	Starts	Wins	Top 5s	Top 10s
1. Ray Guss Jr.	3600	51	24	44	48
2. Joe Kosiski	3600	51	22	39	43
3. Terry Gallaher	3435	43	5	34	40
4. Ed Kosiski	3430	45	8	32	43
5. Dave Chase	3415	46	7	29	44
6. Steve Kosiski	3410	31	8	19	24
7. Kyle Berck	3395	39	6	24	31
8. Gary Webb	3383	28	9	18	20
9. Rollie Frink	3370	37	4	24	28
10. Al Humphrey	3365	49	5	25	34

Pacific Coast Region

Driver	Points	Starts	Wins	Top 5s	Top 10s
1. Ron Bradley	3515	21	16	19	21
2. Steve Hendren	3490	41	11	25	27
3. Gordon Rodgers	3475	22	11	20	22
4. Ken Boyd	3446	22	11	19	21
5. Jeff Silva	3445	43	6	27	34
6. Terry Halverson	3440	23	9	21	22
7. Jim Pettit II	3435	42	8	26	37
8. Brian Balmelli	3425	44	7	28	38
9. Tom Pinkowsky	3425	44	7	28	38
10. Bobby Hogge	3390	37	5	23	26

Eastern Seaboard Region

Driver	Points	Starts	Wins	Top 5s	Top 10s
1. Sean Graham	3570	22	18	21	21
2. David Into	3471	22	12	19	22
3. Freddy Query	3430	22	10	19	22
4. Ron Barfield Jr.	3426	22	11	18	19
5. David Browning Jr.	3392	21	11	17	18
6. Hal McGraw	3339	22	6	17	20
7. Todd Kelley	3310	20	6	17	20
8. Robert Elliott	3261	22	3	15	21
9. Don Smith	3258	22	3	16	21
10. Junior Miller	3236	22	5	14	20

1992 Regional Point Standings

Mid-America Region

Driver	Points	Starts	Wins	Top 5s	Top 10s
1. Larry Phillips	**3600**	**40**	**38**	**38**	**39**
2. Keith Green	3560	41	16	32	37
3. Paul White	3475	36	8	27	31
4. Rodney Harrington	3460	21	9	21	21
5. Billy Sugg	3450	42	7	35	39
6. Charles Ogle	3435	39	6	22	22
7. Bo Rawdon	3435	39	6	31	35
8. Russ Phillips	3435	40	4	33	35
9. Chuck Winders	3430	38	6	27	32
10. Steve Fraise	3365	29	4	21	25

Eastern Seaboard Region

Driver	Points	Starts	Wins	Top 5s	Top 10s
1. Mike Love	3525	22	13	21	21
2. Russell Bernard	3520	22	14	20	21
3. Ron Barfield Jr.	3490	22	15	19	19
4. Edward Wright	3420	22	10	21	22
5. Monk Clary	3420	22	8	19	19
6. Todd Kelley	3378	20	8	19	22
7. Freddie Query	3372	22	10	16	20
8. Ronnie Daniels	3370	22	4	18	20
9. Linwood Arnold	3360	22	3	21	22
10. Robert Elliott	3340	21	3	20	21

Northeast Region

Driver	Points	Starts	Wins	Top 5s	Top 10s
1. Charlie Cragan	3600	40	20	37	40
2. Jerry Marquis	3525	33	13	24	29
3. Glenn Gault	3440	41	7	32	40
4. Rick Miller	3535	38	5	21	36
5. Bob Sibila	3285	40	1	22	35
6. Gerald Gravel	3246	32	1	15	27
7. Tim Ice	3206	28	1	16	25
8. Eric Hudson	3200	32	2	17	24
9. Ed Kennedy	3199	28	2	15	21
10. Buck Catalano	3190	26	2	15	19

Central Region

Driver	Points	Starts	Wins	Top 5s	Top 10s
1. Joe Kosiski	3600	44	20	34	38
2. Ray Guss Jr.	3570	44	17	36	39
3. Steve Boley	3550	44	15	35	39
4. Ed Kosiski	3520	43	13	30	36
5. Kyle Berck	3510	41	11	31	37
6. Jim Swank	3480	39	10	25	34
7. Michael Cothron	3470	41	9	24	33
8. Mark Burgtorf	3430	40	8	24	35
9. Dave Chase	3395	44	7	27	40
10. Rollie Frink	3395	39	3	24	31

Pacific Coast Region

Driver	Points	Starts	Wins	Top 5s	Top 10s
1. Steve Hedren	3600	43	25	34	38
2. Tom Pinkowsky	3520	42	12	34	40
3. Robert Miller	3450	39	9	27	33
4. Randy Olson	3446	21	13	17	21
5. David Philpott	3417	20	10	19	19
6. Eddy McKean	3415	21	9	20	21
7. Darin Fairbanks	3406	22	9	18	22
8. Dan Obrist	3395	30	5	22	24
9. Ed Sans Jr.	3395	40	3	25	34
10. Brian Balmelli	3390	35	6	25	34

Mid-Atlantic Region

Driver	Points	Starts	Wins	Top 5s	Top 10s
1. Michael Ritch	3540	44	14	29	31
2. Bugs Hairfield	3535	33	15	21	25
3. Barry Beggarly	3520	44	12	32	37
4. Johnny Rumley	3505	42	11	32	35
5. Johnny Reynolds	3495	39	11	30	31
6. Jeff Agnew	3480	44	8	35	37
7. Dennis Setzer	3440	30	11	20	24
8. Stacy Compton	3435	38	8	22	27
9. Wayne Patterson	3430	32	7	24	27
10. Jay Fogleman	3340	40	4	21	32

Great Northern Region

Driver	Points	Starts	Wins	Top 5s	Top 10s
1. Steve Murgic	3523	20	17	19	20
2. Kevin Nuttleman	3515	22	13	21	21
3. Craig Raudman	3430	20	8	19	20
4. Jeff Hinkemeyer	3374	20	10	19	19
5. Gary Lewis	3370	22	7	19	19
6. Roger Gannon	3328	22	9	14	22
7. Shawn Pfaff	3306	22	4	17	21
8. Wesley Walton	3295	22	0	21	22
9. Dwain Behrens	3290	22	3	19	22
10. Bobby Hacker	3250	22	2	18	21

Sunbelt Region

Driver	Points	Starts	Wins	Top 5s	Top 10s
1. Ricky Icenhower	3465	22	9	20	21
2. George Hagy	3425	21	10	19	21
3. Mike Goldberry	3407	22	11	17	19
4. Mike Hunter	3372	22	8	19	19
5. John Borneman Jr.	3367	22	10	18	18
6. Paul Banghart	3362	22	7	18	19
7. Dan Beddingfield	3340	22	5	17	21
8. David Showers	3315	22	4	17	21
9. Donny Horelka	3267	22	2	17	19
10. George Walls	3264	22	2	17	20

1995 Regional Point Standings

Pacific Coast Region

Driver	Points	Starts	Wins	Top 5s	Top 10s
1. Larry Phillips	**3650**	**40**	**32**	**38**	**39**
2. Greg Biffle	3650	43	27	34	27
3. David Byrd	3590	44	14	28	32
4. Scott Busby	3535	42	14	28	32
5. David Philpot	3525	37	10	27	34
6. Charles Ogle	3510	22	7	21	22
7. Bobby Hogge IV	3465	42	7	26	33
8. Todd Ellison	3402	26	5	18	24
9. Jim Eaton	3378	21	7	18	20
10. Doug Homer	3340	22	4	20	22

Sunbelt Region

Driver	Points	Starts	Wins	Top 5s	Top 10s
1. Paul White	3560	22	12	21	22
2. Carl Trimmer	3474	21	10	19	19
3. James Littlejohn	3461	22	8	18	20
4. Dennis Andrews	3401	22	6	19	21
5. Don Williams	3400	22	4	18	19
6. Guy Young	3385	22	3	18	22
7. Chris Trickle	3378	22	11	17	19
8. George Bragg	3335	21	5	19	21
9. David Scheidecker	3324	21	8	17	17
10. Rick Johnson	3280	20	4	14	19

1996 Regional Point Standings

Heartland Region

Driver	CPI	Starts	Wins	Top 5s	Top 10s
1. Larry Phillips	**868**	**20**	**14**	**18**	**18**
2. Bill Kimmel	817	20	9	18	19
3. Chuck Winders	754	19	6	11	18
4. John O'Neal Jr.	731	16	12	14	14
5. Donnie Renner	684	21	3	17	20
6. Tim Rauch	599	20	3	17	20
7. Russ Phillips	589	16	3	12	15
8. Kenny Mayden	568	9	4	8	9
9. Brian Ross	556	6	5	6	6
10. Paul Wallen	545	16	2	16	16

Northeast Region

Driver	Points	Starts	Wins	Top 5s	Top 10s
1. John Blewett III	785	21	11	16	17
2. Duane Howard	785	22	2	13	17
3. Jeff Strunk	674	18	3	14	16
4. Bob Arsenberger	672	20	6	17	18
5. Jeff Dunmyer	669	21	7	19	21
6. Ray Swinehart	666	20	3	7	15
7. Dan Koonmen	653	19	6	16	17
8. Rick Wylie	591	16	7	14	14
9. Larry Bond	559	20	2	15	19
10. Gordon Smith	441	11	0	6	10

Atlantic Seaboard Region

Driver	Points	Starts	Wins	Top 5s	Top 10s
1. Wes Troup	839	22	12	17	17
2. BA Wilson	783	20	8	17	20
3. Mike Buffkin	778	21	7	16	19
4. Eddie Johnson	755	21	8	14	17
5. Donnie Apple	754	24	11	20	21
6. Charles Powell III	742	21	8	17	18
7. Grady Moss	697	20	8	17	18
8. Barry Beggarly	695	22	7	19	19
9. Robert Elliott	622	21	7	21	21
10. Jamey Lee	536	21	1	17	20

Blue Ridge Region

Driver	Points	Starts	Wins	Top 5s	Top 10s
1. Steven Howard	796	21	14	19	19
2. Andy Kirby	778	24	8	16	19
3. Scott Kirby	713	19	9	17	17
4. Martin Nesbitt	672	22	7	20	21
5. Dexter Canipe	644	23	4	16	21
6. Jeff Agnew	642	22	9	20	22
7. Tim Brown	622	20	1	9	15
8. Chad Harris	600	23	2	15	20
9. Randy Ratliff	556	22	5	18	22
10. Tony Willis	414	12	2	9	12

Midwest Region

Driver	Points	Starts	Wins	Top 5s	Top 10s
1. Steve Boley	778	21	7	12	20
2. Joe Kosiski	762	20	8	16	18
3. Ed Kosiski	736	18	7	13	16
4. Jeff Wildung	645	20	8	14	17
5. Mark Wyman	613	17	9	15	16
6. Jeff Aikey	572	17	3	16	17
7. Denny Eckrich	557	19	4	13	17
8. Dwayne Clarke	536	24	7	23	24
9. Tom Svoboda	475	16	1	10	15
10. Larry Brockman	292	10	2	10	10

Pacific Coast Region

Driver	Points	Starts	Wins	Top 5s	Top 10s
1. Bobby Hogge IV	797	24	14	21	22
2. Dick Shephard	767	20	6	17	19
3. Jerry Gay	670	20	6	19	20
4. Roger Gannon	648	22	11	19	22
5. Dave Byrd	623	23	6	20	21
6. James Busby	620	21	3	8	12
7. Kevin Riniker	614	21	6	19	21
8. Kenny Nott	595	22	2	13	19
9. Brandon Kaeding	584	13	3	11	13
10. Jim Pettit II	534	10	3	8	9

Great West Region

Driver	CPI	Starts	Wins	Top 5s	Top 10s
1. Eddy McKean	777	20	13	20	20
2. Bruce Yackey	717	20	3	14	17
3. Todd Ellison	704	21	13	21	21
4. Mike Obrist	645	23	7	18	20
5. Tom Moriarity	629	22	2	16	20
6. Brad Rhoads	615	20	10	16	20
7. Jeff Byrd	605	21	9	21	21
8. Doug Homer	585	22	9	21	22
9. Kevin Bumberger	538	18	1	8	16
10. Jerry Langbraaten	537	21	2	18	20

MidAmerica Region

Driver	Points	Starts	Wins	Top 5s	Top 10s
1. Mike VanSparrentak	788	22	8	19	20
2. Richard Wateski	715	22	5	14	20
3. Todd Bennett	708	19	7	12	18
4. Jeff Martin	689	20	3	19	19
5. Shannon Babb	643	19	6	15	17
6. Brian Johnson	632	20	10	19	20
7. Bobby Wilberg	632	20	7	17	19
8. Terry Gallaher	545	15	7	15	15
9. Robert Hansberry	464	10	5	9	9
10. Mark Burgtorf	450	10	3	8	10

Sunbelt Region

Driver	Points	Starts	Wins	Top 5s	Top 10s
1. Carl Trimmer	833	22	11	19	19
2. Mike Love	801	23	16	22	23
3. Paul White	759	23	10	22	23
4. David Browning Jr.	733	21	9	20	21
5. Mike Fitch	687	20	5	17	19
6. Jimmy Littlejohn	683	22	7	17	21
7. Donnie Bazemore	679	22	5	16	21
8. Marvin Lough	673	19	3	12	16
9. Mike Ray	657	24	10	20	23
10. Donny Horelka	639	20	6	15	20

New England Region

Driver	Points	Starts	Wins	Top 5s	Top 10s
1. Dale Planck	743	20	7	12	15
2. Mitch Gibbs	719	20	5	15	17
3. Ted Christopher	683	16	4	10	13
4. Bobby Gahan	673	19	8	17	18
5. Mike Maiettan Sr.	660	20	2	12	17
6. Charles Steuer	652	20	3	12	17
7. William Bry	642	19	4	16	19
8. Richard Houlihan	639	15	3	12	15
9. Thomas Quinney	638	16	7	11	13
10. David Berube	626	19	2	10	15

Source: NASCAR

ACKNOWLEDGEMENTS

There are some people we would like to thank because truly, without them, their passion and commitment to this project, this book would not have been possible.

First and foremost, we'd like to thank Judy Phillips. From the start Judy has been an inspiration and we appreciate everything she has done to assist us. We're glad we will always be able to call her our friend.

We'd also like to thank Terry Phillips. He allowed us to interview him during a time when he was busy with his own racing career. We appreciate his contributions because he was able to give us insight into the relationship as father and son and how much they cared for one another.

Kathie Zeszutek has also been a driving force to help keep the project moving along. She helped in so many ways that we cannot thank her enough for her true devotion to the project.

We also owe a huge debt of gratitude to Paul Schaefer of NASCAR. He was onboard before we ever began writing. We found his enthusiasm contagious and he helped launch the project, offering guidance and sage advice from the start. He also took time from his extremely busy schedule to help us and for that, we will always be indebted.

We would like to thank Dan Mahoney for providing us with many of the photos used in the book. They helped us tell the story and provided many memories for us and anyone who reads the book. Dan has lots of great photos that can be seen online at www.mahoneyphotos.com.

Cynthia Clayton Chandler spent countless hours transcribing interviews. By doing so, she saved us time and effort that allowed us to move on to other areas to keep the project moving. Thanks Cindy; you are awesome!

We would also like to thank the Ozarks Area Racing Association for the preservation of the history of racing in the Ozarks. They were able to provide photographs and information that we needed to complete the book.

Cheryl Blair and Cheryl Correll of First Impressions Printing in Springfield, Missouri, graciously designed the book cover concept. These two ladies worked tirelessly without complaining even after we asked them to tweak their design several times. Check out their website at www.fiprinting.net.

We would also like to thank the following NASCAR Sprint Car drivers who took time out of the schedules to speak with us about Larry Phillips and the impact he had on their careers: Mark Martin, Ken Schrader, Kenny Wallace and Rusty Wallace.

And a special thanks to the Missouri Sports Hall of Fame for allowing us to take photographs and view memorabilia and historic artifacts from its Larry Phillips collection.

There are many more people who we would like to recognize for their valuable contributions to the book. We can't thank you enough for sharing with us your fond memories of Larry Phillips:

Ray Batson
Bob Beeter
Tim Belk
Trenton Berry
Steve Brallier
Bill Breshears
Terry Brumley
James Chism
Roger Chism
Rodney Combs
Kevin Fletcher
Lester Friebe
Jim Hunter
Charles and Virginia Hurley
Dennis Huth
James Ince
Bobby Menzie
Randy Mooneyham
Joe Naegler
Bob Nelson
Tommy Joe Pauchert
Mark Perry
Ned Reynolds
Dale Roper
Lynn Sanders
Rick Sharp
Brent Slane
Dennis Slane
Lyndal Scranton
Roger Wasson
Earnie Watson
Bob and Loretta Williams

We also want to thank our agent, Jay Poynor, for his tireless efforts at marketing the book to a publisher. We sincerely appreciate all of your hard work.

And we owe a debt of gratitude to our publicist, Barbara Martin. She never tires of scheduling appearances and book signings on our behalf. Thank Barbara; we truly appreciate all of your effort.

We would be remiss if we did not thank our publisher, Bella Rosa Books. Rod Hunter and his staff put up with numerous additions and other changes in the middle of the publishing process without complaining. Thank you for all of your hard work and for making the dream a reality.

We have tried to include everyone but, without fail, there is bound to be a name or two we have omitted. Please be assured that any omission was unintended and we thank you for anything you have done to help us with the book.

And of course we want to thank the readers who, by purchasing a book, make a contribution to the Larry Phillips Foundation. Part of the proceeds go to this worthy organization that will continue to make Larry Phillips a winner forever by providing scholarship funds and medical funds for those in need. The Foundation's Web site is www.larryphillipsfoundation.org.

Thank you all and we hope you have as much enjoyment reading this book as we did putting it all together.

Kendall Bell
David Zeszutek

Dan Mahoney collection

Larry Phillips holds a trophy in the inspection area after winning a race.

About the Authors

Kendall Bell

Kendall Bell is an award-winning journalist who has won more than twenty awards from the South Carolina Press Association, the Associated Press and others. He is a native South Carolinian and veteran reporter having worked at *The Charlotte Observer, The* (Myrtle Beach) *Sun News, The Lancaster News* and as an editor at *The Beaufort Gazette and The* (Sumter, SC) *Item.*

Bell's writing credits include two anthologies, *From the Heart: Stories of Love and Friendship* (Coastal Villages Press, 2003) *and From the Heart 2: More Stories of Love and Friendship* (Coastal Villages Press, 2004). He has also been published in numerous magazines including *Writer's Digest, South Carolina Sheriff, Lowcountry Monthly Magazine, Hilton Head Island Monthly Magazine, Sandlapper Magazine* and others. Bell is in the process of writing a mystery series. He is in growing demand nationally as a speaker who is known for his unique wit and humor. He has developed workshops for beginning writers as well as advanced workshops for published authors. Bell is presently working toward a master's degree in military history.

He lives in South Carolina with his cat, Scooby. His website is www.kendallbell.com.

David Zeszutek

David Zeszutek has been a native of Springfield, Missouri, for more than fifty years. He attended Missouri State University and Drury University in Springfield. He has been in the banking industry for twenty-five years. David was first introduced to Larry Phillips in the sixties while attending races at the Fairgrounds Speedway in Springfield with his mom and dad. Ever since, he had been a fan and was intrigued by the number 75 car winning much of the time. Later, during his teenage years, David got to know Larry by going to his shop on Commercial Street in Springfield. In his adult life,

David worked on several projects with Larry. David wrote this book to help preserve the history and impact that Larry had on the sport.

David created the Larry Phillips Foundation to keep Larry's name alive and to help people with catastrophic illnesses and to provide scholarships for students. For more information or to make a tax-deductible contribution, go online to www.larryphillipsfoundation.org or send it to the Larry Phillips Foundation, Post Office Box 5063, Springfield, MO 65801.

David owns Race Won Consulting and works for a local financial institution. He lives in Springfield with his wife, Kathie.

Notes from the Authors

David Zeszutek: The seeds of desire for writing this book began when I was a youngster attending races with my family.

It started back in 1968, when my mother and father took me to my first race at the Fairgrounds Speedway in Springfield. I can still recall to this day there were a lot of cars checked into the pits. They had heat races first, and that was the first time I saw the number 75 car of Larry Phillips. He ended up winning the feature race that day from the tailback position. He had a way of moving in and out of traffic that I have never seen before or since. My father and I became instant fans. Through the years I went to many races with my mother and father and got to see a lot of memorable moments in stock car racing. Those memories are now my fondest of that number 75 car.

In my teen years, when I was beginning to drive a car myself, my friend, Kelly Bench and I traveled to many of Larry's races throughout the country. We spent many hours at the shop with him and helped with the race car. He gave us sodas. I was amazed at Larry's work ethic and how intense he was when he was preparing for the next race.

Later in my life, I worked at a bank in Springfield and also owned a racing collectible business called Davey's Race Place. We had three locations and also sold merchandise at the race tracks. We designed and sold Larry Phillips T-shirts. In doing so, I got to know Larry better as a friend and really enjoyed my time with him.

My strongest reason for writing this book was not just because I was a fan. It was because my dad, Ted, was his biggest fan. He suffered a stroke in 1993, a year after my mother died. My wife and I began selling collectibles at the tracks and my dad would go along. He enjoyed speaking with all the race fans. But most of all he was there to watch Larry Phillips win. My dad had a special relationship with Larry. He could talk with him and joke like no one ever could. Larry was always kind and respectful to my father. I really appreciated this time that Larry gave my Dad. This relationship kept him active for many years after his stroke up until his death in December 2002. Nothing has ever compared to watching and working with Larry Phillips at the race tracks.

Kendall Bell: I first met David in 1990 when friends Larry and Cindy Roach invited me to come along on a trip to visit their family in Springfield. While there, Larry and I decided to visit Lebanon I-44 Speedway in Lebanon, Missouri. That turned out to be the only time I actually saw Larry Phillis race in person. Of course it was a race that Larry won.

While at the track, I noticed a young couple selling racing collectibles and struck up a conversation. That couple was David and Kathie Zeszutek.

As the years passed, we became close friends. The three of us visited several NASCAR tracks in the Southeast together, including Charlotte, Bristol, Darlington and Rockingham.

During one of those visits, David asked me about writing Larry's biography. At first, I must admit I was a little reluctant. Having just released my second book at the time, I knew all too well how much work would be required. And the fact that David and I lived more than 1,000 miles apart wouldn't make it any easier.

A few months later, I thought David had forgotten about it. He had not. The next time he brought it up was in June 2006. I happened to have a meeting scheduled with my literary agent for the following week in New York City. I said that, if my agent, Jay Poynor, would agree to represent us, I'd do it. Otherwise, I needed to concentrate on writing mysteries—which has been my desire for several years.

The following week while dining with Jay at a fine restaurant on Manhattan's Lower East Side, I pitched the idea, expecting him to say no. Instead, he agreed. And within a week, the contracts were signed and thus began a fifty-five month journey that ended with the publication of this book.

LARRY PHILLIPS

JULY 3, 1942 - SEPTEMBER 21, 2004

CPSIA information can be obtained at www.ICGtesting.com
Printed in the USA
241683LV00003B/32/P

9 781933 523958